Through the Eyes of Faith

2nd Edition

Compiled by
Dr. Jack E. Bower, CPA
Eastern University
Associate Professor of Accounting
Chair, Division of the Social Services
Chair, Department of Business

Published by
Profitable Publishing
A Division of Thornton Publishing, Inc

The photograph on the cover is a statue of Saint Thomas Aquinas who is quite possibility the father of modern accounting. Prior to the life of Saint Thomas Aquinas accounting was a mathematical discipline concerned with counting things of value. During and after the life of Saint Thomas accounting became a social science focused on the logic of how things of value related to each other and the critical question of a just profit. Chapter three will address this topic in more detail. Permission to photograph the statue was granted by Reverend Lawrence F. Crehan, Pastor of St. Thomas Aquinas Church, 601 Bristol Pike, Croydon PA. 19021, the background was edited by Marguerite Reed-Brooke, Administrative Assistant, Department of Business, Eastern University.

Proudly Printed & Publishedin the USA by
Profitable Publishing
a Division of Thornton Publishing, Inc
6834 S. University Blvd. #416
Littleton, CO 80122

1-303-794-8888

www.BooksToBelieveIn.com   www.ProfitablePublishing.net

publisher@profitablepublishing.net

ISBN: 0-9723309-0-9

Table of Contents

PART IV – Accounting and Moral Philosophy

DISCLAIMER

Accounting Through the Eyes of Faith is an anthology of chapters written by Christian accountants and compiled by Dr. Jack E. Bower of Eastern University. This book was **not done** in collaboration or sponsorship with the Council of Christian Colleges & Universities; nor did it receive assistance in any manner or form from the Council of Christian Colleges & Universities, which discontinued a series of books with a similar title and theme published by Harper Collins Publishers.

ADVISORY BOARD

The Eastern University accounting faculty served as the Advisory Board for compiling the second edition. Members of the Advisory Board are as follows:

Jack E. Bower, CPA, Chair
Jeffrey J. Davis, CPA, CMA
Mary Jo Jones, CPA
Robin Lowery, CPA

Those wishing to submit chapters for the third edition should contact Professor Bower for details. Chapters do not necessarily represent the views of the complier, the advisory board, or Eastern University. Responsibility for opinions expressed and accuracy of facts rests solely with the author(s) of each chapter.

PREFACE
Scriptural Admonition
to Study Accounting
Luke 16:1-13

Jesus told his disciples:

> *"There was a rich man whose manager was accused of wasting his possessions. So he called him in and asked him, what is this I hear about you? Give an account of your management, because you cannot be manager any longer."*
>
> *The manager said to himself; 'What shall I do now? My master is taking away my job, I'm not strong enough to dig and I'm ashamed to beg. I know what I'll do so that when I lose my job here, people will welcome me into their houses.'*
>
> *So he called in each of his master's debtors. He said to the first, 'How much do you owe my master?' 'Eight hundred gallons of olive oil, he replied.' The manager told him, 'Take your bill, sit down **quickly**, and make it four hundred.'*
>
> *Then he asked the second, 'And how much do you owe?' 'A thousand bushels of wheat,'he replied. He told him to 'Take your bill and make it eight hundred.'*
>
> *The master commended the dishonest manager because he had acted shrewdly. For the people of this world are more shrewd in dealing with their own kind than are the people of light."*

Jesus makes the observation that shrewd business practices are sometimes not used by believers in God (people of light). Accounts receivable discounting is now standard business practice and terms like 2/10 net 30 are in common use today. Note that the stronger discount included the word "quickly." This passage and the story in Luke 19:23 imply recognition of the time value of money (NPV), but the real substance of this story is in the relationship between the physical and the spiritual world that follows. Continuing with verse 9:

For I tell you, use worldly wealth to gain friends for yourselves, so that when it is gone, you will be welcomed into eternal dwellings.

Who does the manager of accounts receivable represent and who is the master or owner of the estate? I suggest that we are the manager in the story, the stewards of God's creation. The master is God and we are encouraged to give away the physical things that are under our control. We store-up treasure in heaven by being generous with the wealth God has given us to manage, and at the same time we please those who are in debt to God. Humanity is often depicted as being in **debt** to God. This is why Jesus said he was our year of Jubilee (Leviticus 25 & Luke 4:19-21). Through Him our debts are forgiven. More about this topic in chapter two. Now the scriptural admonition to study accounting.

Whoever can be trusted with very little can also be trusted with much, and whoever is dishonest with very little will also be dishonest with much.

What is the little and what is the much? I suggest that the physical world is the little and the spiritual world is the much. Control over the seduction of physical possessions is critical to receiving spiritual property (a man's life does not consist of the abundance of his possessions, Luke 12:13-21).

So if you have not been trustworthy in handling worldly wealth, who will trust you with true riches? And if you have not been trustworthy with someone else's property, who will give you property of your own?

The *Accounting Through the Eyes of Faith* is dedicated to the trustworthy handling of worldly wealth. This passage gives strong admonition to study accounting. The main point of the parable; **Manage the wealth He has given to you, in a trustworthy manner**

and you can be a manager of God's spiritual property.

> *No servant can serve two masters, Either he will hate the one and love the other, or he will be devoted to the one and despise the other. You cannot serve both God and Money.*

Yours in Him,
Dr. Jack E. Bower, CPA

Part I

Introduction

THE LIBERAL ARTS AND YOUR VOCATION

By

Jack E. Bower, C.P.A., Ph.D.
Associate Professor of Accounting
&
Frederick J. Boehlke, Jr., Ph.D.
Professor of History
Eastern University

One of the more frequently asked questions among college students is, "Why do we have to take courses like 'Justice in a Pluralistic Society' or 'Science, Technology, and Values'? The implication is that the "liberal arts" are a waste of time and that only studies in a "major" like accounting will provide the ability to secure a job. The question deserves a proper response considering the cost of a college education and the fact that the liberal arts or core represents about 46%[1] of the total course work required for a bachelor's degree. The following will help explain what it means to receive a liberal arts education.

The liberal arts were first defined during the early middle Ages in a book titled, *Marriage of Mercury and Philology* by Martianus Capella. The marriage of these two gods occurred on the Milky Way with the other gods as witnesses. Originally, the seven liberal arts were: Grammar, Rhetoric (effective public speaking), Dialectic (debate) representing the literary arts; Arithmetic, Geometry (including surveying), Astronomy and Music representing the mathematical sciences.[2] It is important to note that these were the "vocational subjects for the clergy."[3] A priest needed the literary skills for sermons, arithmetic to keep the accounting records (accounting was soon to be included in all math textbooks), geometry to settle boundary disputes between farmers, astronomy to set the ecclesiastical calendar and music for worship. **The seven original liberal arts had a vocational focus**.

During the Renaissance, the focus was on a reconciliation of Plato and Aristotle. The effort was actually begun during the Middle

Ages by Boethius, a Roman patrician, who held the office of consul under Theodoric the Ostrogoth.[4] There were two domains: the world of Plato, which was a domain of ideas (truth, love, et al.) and the world of Aristotle, which was the domain of the physical and observable (heat, light, et al.). St. Thomas Aquinas, who lived between 1225 and 1275, brought the two worlds together. You may have heard the expression that St. Thomas Aquinas baptized Aristotle.

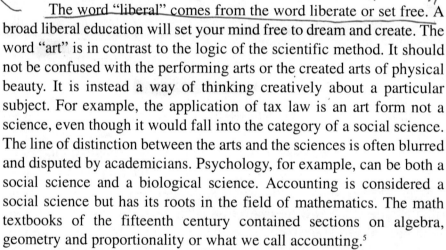

It was believed that a properly educated person of the Renaissance could operate in both domains. The college student who does well academically and is also skilled in mechanical repairs (fixing a car, for example) as well as playing some musical instrument would be called a "true Renaissance" man or woman. Their broad general education allows them to participate in both the physical world and the world of thoughts and ideas.

The word "liberal" comes from the word liberate or set free. A broad liberal education will set your mind free to dream and create. The word "art" is in contrast to the logic of the scientific method. It should not be confused with the performing arts or the created arts of physical beauty. It is instead a way of thinking creatively about a particular subject. For example, the application of tax law is an art form not a science, even though it would fall into the category of a social science. The line of distinction between the arts and the sciences is often blurred and disputed by academicians. Psychology, for example, can be both a social science and a biological science. Accounting is considered a social science but has its roots in the field of mathematics. The math textbooks of the fifteenth century contained sections on algebra, geometry and proportionality or what we call accounting.[5]

Today a liberal arts education is thought of as a general education including a specialization or what we call a major. Two centuries ago this was not the case. Only the subjects of Philosophy, Latin, English and Mathematics were part of a general education.[6] Actually, the specific courses that constitute a general education have always been and continue to be a disputable topic in educational circles. The evolving debate and the resulting curriculum modifications provide considerable insight into the nature of what we call a liberal arts education. The rest of this article will briefly highlight some of the discussion in a historical context.

Here is an example of the discussion from the Self-Study Committee of Lawrence College as recorded by the *Carnegie Series in American Education: The Search of a Common Learning*:

*"Liberal education **must include** an exploration, in some depth, of at least one area of knowledge which may be determined by the student's own personal interests **or by vocational needs**. Such an exploration, they add, a general education cannot provide; since at best, it can only give an introduction to the broad areas of knowledge from which further exploration must follow."*[7]

The debate of a general education not requiring a specialization to requiring one, progressed slowly over time at colleges around the world.

Medieval education was indoctrination. The goal was to mold the mind into a fixed type.[8] The Renaissance changed all of that and a liberal education was an education of reason and logic intended to dispel superstition and fear. "In the fifteenth and sixteenth centuries the scholars of the Renaissance turned from theological education to human letters."[9] The study of the literature of antiquity and languages became the backbone of the liberal arts, what we label the humanities.

By the early eighteen hundreds, a general college education included two courses of study, the classics and the sciences. The core curriculum was defined as: math, language, physical science, biological science, philosophy, religion and history. The longest of the courses of study was in the physical sciences.[10] The social sciences were not included even though their existence was firmly established. The thinking of this time was that the specializations such as law, medicine or divinity should be limited to graduate schools. It is true that graduate schools significantly refine and develop specific areas of knowledge. The problem is that many careers do not require a graduate education so the debate over the inclusion of specializations in a bachelor degree program continued. The debate took a different form at each college. A brief history of the University of Pennsylvania will illustrate the progressive development of the debate.

The great college founders included names like Benjamin Franklin, University of Pennsylvania; John Harvard, Harvard University; and Elihu Yale of Yale University. Some of the founders, such as Benjamin Franklin, wanted a very practical and utilitarian type of education. Franklin's views on education did not prevail however, and it was a source of great bitterness and conflict for him.[11] His proposed curriculum was mathematics, geography, history, logic, and natural and moral philosophy. "It should be an education for citizenship, and should lead to mercantile and civic success and usefulness."[12] His proposed curriculum was never tested. The trustees of the academy were the most prominent men of the city and the curriculum followed the traditional format of British Schools having a Philosophical School, a Latin School, an English School and a Mathematical School.[13] The next to be added were the History and Writing Schools.

These key liberal arts' courses were considered the "tools of learning." Once learned, the tools could then be applied to various subjects. For example, Latin was a study of structure and expression. All of the subjects focused on the construction of an argument and how to defend it. Educated persons were articulate (Rhetoric) and able to debate a topic (Dialectic). Many scholars of the twentieth century insist we have lost these tools of learning in our general education requirements.[14]

The University of Pennsylvania (U of P) dates its beginnings to the year 1746; the first property was purchased in May of 1740. This date places U of P before either Princeton or Columbia. All of the colleges of this time period suffered financial difficulties from 1791 to 1828. "This was not a great academic age."[15] The colleges that faired the best during these times were the ones with a specific church base or denominational focus. What turned the U of P around was specialization. The Medical School and Law School were added in 1791, which increased the enrollment while the liberal arts' departments declined in faculty and students. Other specializations were also added in music, business, dentistry and several other fields. It is interesting to note that history became a neglected subject in the liberal arts during this time period, but was eventually restored.[16]

What does the history of the U of P teach us? The paradigm of a solely liberal arts' education failed. To function in our modern industrial society requires some degree of specialization. In other words, it takes both. A strong general education should include a specialization and together they produce a well-educated person. The dominant accrediting agency for business schools (AACSB) requires that the general education requirement comprises at least 50% of the curriculum. The blending of the two is what makes the American educational system so valued internationally. Various studies, such as Workplace 2000, confirm this conclusion:

"The literate person in the year 2000 will have to be both technically and socially competent. That means that engineers must have an understanding of cultural anthropology and an appreciation of literature, and the English majors need to be skilled with the personal computer and understand science and technology."[17]

A discussion of the significance of the liberal arts should not imply that the specializations are of a lower academic heritage. The study of subjects like music or business principles are as old as the history of mankind yet were not considered a part of the liberal arts' core in the 1800's. The pyramids, a managerial masterpiece, were constructed eleven hundred years before Joseph was sold by his brothers as a slave to the Ishmaelites headed towards Egypt. The oldest known written documents are inventory records recorded on clay tablets. Pope Leo X appointed the first professor of accounting in 1514 at the Sapienza in Rome. This was the highest university of learning in all of Christendom.[18]

Respect for a discipline should come from its lineage and the service that it provides to society. Modern accounting, like classical music, finds its roots in the Renaissance. St. Thomas Aquinas with his refinement of the analogy (Greek="analogos" from which we get our word proportionate) inspired the mathematics discipline of proportionality (double-entry accounting.) Double-entry accounting has been used for over 700 years and has a long history of distinguished professors and scholars teaching mathematics and accounting at various universities all over Europe.[19] Compare this to the development of the natural sciences before the last 200 years. For example, Professor Charles Morton of Harvard (two hundred years ago) was teaching that the annual migration of birds is around the moon, a journey of 200,000 miles in two months flying through space.[20] Many of the specializations like accounting have a heritage or lineage that extends far beyond even the recognition of the liberal arts in the middle Ages.

Our curriculum will teach you to think critically and to truly appreciate the world around you. We will challenge you intellectually in both the general education courses and in the specialization. Most of all, we hope to strengthen your faith so that you can know and express to others the things you believe about God. Welcome to the world of academia!

Bibliography

Bechel, Paul M. Wheaton College, A Heritage Remembered
    1860-1984. Harold Shaw Publishing, Wheaton,
    Illinois, 1984.

Bell, Daniel. The Reforming of General Education, Columbia
    U. Press, N.Y., 1966.

Cheyney, Edward Potts. History of the University of
    Pennsylvania, U. of Penn Press, Philadelphia, PA., 1940.

Dyer, John P. Ivory Towers in the Market Place, Bobbs
    Merrill Co., N.Y., 1956.

Kenny, Anthony. The Five Ways, St. Thomas Aquinas'
    Proofs of God's Existence, University of Notre Dame Press, 1969.

Geijsbeck, John B. Ancient Double-Entry Bookkeeping,
    Scholars Book Co., Houston,
    TX, 1914.

Howard, Harold C. Provost's Perspective on Higher
    Education in the 21st Century. Eastern
    College, PA., 1997.

Journal of Accounting Research, spring 1973, 47-61 &
    Abacus, December 1973,
    137-155 & Nottingham Medieval Studies, Vol. XVI, 1972.

LaMonte, John L. The World of The Middle Ages, Appleton
    Century-Crofts, N.Y., 1949.

Littleton, A.C. Accounting Evolution, U. of Alabama Press,
    American Institute
    Publishing Co., N.Y., 1981.

Martin, Everett Dean. The Meaning of a Liberal Education,
    WW Norton & Co., N.Y., N.Y., 1926.

Nobes, Christopher. The Development of Double Entry, Garland Publishing, Inc., N.Y., 1984.

Oakley, Francis. Community of Learning, the American College and the Liberal Arts Tradition, Oxford U. Press, N.Y., 1992.

Peragallo, Edward. Origin and Evolution of Double Entry Bookkeeping, A study of Italian Practice from the Fourteenth Century, American Institute Publishing Co., 1939.

Sayers, Dorothy L. The Lost Tools of Learning, Methuen & Co., London, 1948.

Thomas, Russell. The Search for a Common Learning: General Education, 1800-1960, McGraw-Hill Book Co., N.Y., 1962.

[1] The Eastern University Fixed Core is 24 plus the Breadth Requirements of 34; 24+34/127=.45669

[2] The World of the Middle Ages, by LaMonte, John L., page 81.

[3] Ibid, page 81.

[4] Ibid, page 82.

[5] The Development of Double Entry, Nobes, Christopher.

[6] The Search for a Common Learning: General Education, 1800-1960, Thomas, Russell, McGraw-Hill Book Co. Inc. 1962, page 3.

[7] ibid, page 4.

[8] The meaning of a Liberal Education, Martin, Everett Dean. W.W.Norton & Co. Inc. N.Y., 1926, page 32.

[9] ibid, page 33.

[10] The Search for a Common Learning, Thomas, Russell, page 15.

[11] History of the University of Pennsylvania 1740 - 1940, Cheyney, Edward Potts. U of P press, 1940, page 29.

[12] Ibid, page 29.

[13] Ibid, page 72.

[14] The Lost Tools of Learning, Sayers, Dorothy, Methuen & Co. of London, 1948.

[15] History of the University of Pennsylvania, Cheyney, page 176.

[16] Ibid, page 242.

[17] The Virtual Corporation: Structuring and Revitalizing the Corporation for the 21st Century, Davidow, William & Michael Malone, NY Harper Business, 1992, pages 259 & 260 Taken from Provost's Perspective, by Howard, Harold, Eastern College, 1997.

[18] Accounting Evolution to 1900, Littleton, A.C., U of Alabama Press, 1981, page 3.

[19] Grammateus, a German professor, 1518; Jerome Cardan, 1539, Professor at Pavia and later at Bologna.

[20] Bid, page 5.

Part II

Accounting's Spiritual Roots

HEAVENLY ACCOUNTING

By
Dr. Jack E. Bower
Eastern University

Introduction

No human being can comprehend the majesty and wisdom of God. Does a perfect God with an infallible memory keep a general ledger? Of course not, but just like the "streets of gold" God uses the imagery of keeping books to help us understand His relationship with mankind. "Heavenly Accounting" gives some insight into how God would do it if, in fact, God did keep books in the way that we finite humans understand double-entry accounting.

The entity concept is the first struggle of using the scriptural references to accounting terminology. The scriptures were written from God's perspective, and therefore; the accounting references are to God's accounting equation. Abraham's faith (credit) reduced his accounts receivable. We want to read the scriptures from the perspective of their own spiritual accounting equation. In an individual (entity) equation, perhaps faith would be the owner's equity and the fruits of the spirit would be the assets.

Justice and Love

The God of the Christian faith is a God of justice and love. Justice means God must punish sin. Love is His desire to forgive us. These two qualities present a dilemma for a perfect God when establishing a contractual relationship with a less than perfect mankind. God didn't create the universe with this paradox. The dilemma or impasse in the relationship was a result of mankind's violation of specific provisions of God's covenant with them (Gen. 2:16,17). The details of the violation are described in Genesis chapter three. Here is a brief outline from an accounting perspective.

Assets = Grace

When God created the world it was a perfect place free of intentional irregularities, and God could freely interact with His creation in a mode of love. The accounting equation was simply; the assets of heaven and earth = the grace of God, His net worth in creation. Mankind, through interaction with God's major competitor Satan, broke the terms of the contract with God the Creator. Mankind was forced to vacate the premises of Eden and to enter a less than desirable work environment.

"Cursed is the ground because of you; through painful
toil you will eat of it all the days of your life.
It will produce thorns and thistles for you and you
will eat the plants of the field. By the sweat of
your brow you will eat your food until you return to
the ground since from it you were taken;" Gen. 3:17ff

The eviction notice was not sufficient restitution for the intentional violation on the part of mankind. This violation meant that the status of mankind with God changed. God reclassified man from the most significant part of the inventory of creation "God created man in his own image" (Gen. 1:27), to an accounts receivable. After the reclassification, mankind was now accountable for every minor violation; even every careless word spoken is charged to an account for each member of humanity (Matt 12:36). With mankind's violation of the contract a new element entered the accounting equation, "sin", a liability account for God to repay. Equating sin with debt is well documented in the scriptures. In the words of Jesus "Forgive us our debts as we also have forgiven our debtors" Matthew 6:12.

$$\text{Assets} = \text{Sin} + \text{Grace}$$

The Lord replied to Moses. Whoever has sinned
*against me I will blot out of my **book***...*
However when the time comes for me to punish,
I will punish them for their sins." Exodus 32:33f

*"But I tell you that men will have to give **account***
on the day of judgment for every careless word
they have spoken." Matt 12:36

*"So then, each of us will give **an account** of himself to God."* Romans 14:12

*"And I saw the dead, great and small, standing before the throne, and **books** were opened. Another **book** was opened, which is the **book of life.*** The dead were judged according to what they had done as recorded in **the books.**"* Revelation 20:12

*SIDEBAR - Notice that there are two ledgers for humanity's accounts receivable. One special or subsidiary ledger is the "Book of Life" and the other is simply called "The Books". (More about this point later.)

Back to the two qualities of God, justice and love. This is the dilemma for God. The justice quality of God required a proper payment for the violation of the contract called sin, but the love quality of God wants to forgive the violation and interact freely with mankind. Of course, the violations have continued in an exponential manner as mankind has multiplied and treated each other wrongly and therefore sinned against God.

Does mankind earn any credits against each individual account receivable? Yes, God is compared to a king who wants to settle the accounts of His servants (Matt 18:23ff). The story told by Jesus concerns a debtor who is forgiven a large debt but is unwilling to forgive even a small debt owed to him. As each person forgives the debt of others they establish credit with God against the debits of their violations (James 5:20).

The journal entry for sin:

	Dr.	Cr.
Accounts Receivable	XXX	
Sin		XXX

The journal entry for good deeds and forgiveness of others:

Grace	XXX	
Accounts Receivable		XXX

Can good deeds and good thoughts fully repay the accounts receivable of each person? This key question was the principle subject of two books by the apostle Paul: Romans and Galatians. (These were best sellers of their times.) In these books, Paul argues very effectively that no one can be declared paid in full by human deeds alone. Paul uses the example of Abraham, who was the father of their nation and known as an extremely righteous man. In other words, if the person with the greatest good deeds and good thoughts in Jewish history couldn't do it, than no one can. It was the **faith** of Abraham that was **credited** to his account, not his good deeds (Gen. 15:6).

The journal entry for Abraham's faith was:

	Dr.	Cr.
Grace	XXX	
Accounts Receivable		XXX

Many faith groups argue that it is a Biblical principle that good deeds cover sin. Therefore, faithful church attendance will score some points with God; sort of like punching a spiritual time clock. Interestingly, certain good deeds will even cover a multitude of sins.

"Remember this: Whoever turns a sinner from the error of his way will save him from death and cover over a multitude of sins."
James 5:20.

The key question is this. Are good deeds enough to pay for ALL sin? Does a just God need to punish mankind who has more debits than credits? The answer is YES! The most convincing story of the principle that good deeds are never enough is told by Jesus in Matt 19. A wealthy young man comes to Jesus and asks what is necessary for eternal life. Jesus gives him the check list: Thou shall not ...... Certainly Jesus thought he would get the point, but he did not. "All these I have kept", the young man said. "What do I still lack?". Okay Jesus said, "If you want to be perfect, go sell your possessions and give to the poor, and you will have treasure in heaven. Then come, follow me." The man left very sad because he had substantial investments. The disciples asked, "Who then can be saved?" Jesus looked at them and said.

"With man this is impossible, but with God all things are possible." Matt 19:16ff

How was God going to reconcile the books and draw man back to Himself? This was a complex problem in logic that even Satan couldn't unravel until it actually happened. God, who wants to forgive the debits, can't because of His basic quality of justice. Mankind wants to have the account paid but can't earn enough credits to justify the account.

How God would solve this dilemma was the greatest mystery story of all time, one that baffled Jewish theologians and Satan for centuries (Eph. 3:5). God's answer was to have the accounts of humanity cleared by a transfer to the account of someone without sin. Someone with so large a credit balance that the debits of all of humanity couldn't wipe out that balance. Jesus Christ was the answer, a mystery hidden throughout the centuries. Here was the perfect person who could become sin for all of mankind, thereby reconciling God to mankind.

How did Jesus obtain so large a credit balance? Did Jesus have a credit balance as a result of His involvement in creation?

"Through him all things were made; without him nothing was made that has been made." John 1:3

	Dr.	Cr.
Heaven and Earth	XXX	
Jesus Christ		XXX

Did this credit balance stay with Him as he was reclassified from Godhead to a part of humanity? This is an interesting accounting question. This passage in Phil 2:6 would argue no, but the passage in Col. 2:9 would argue yes.

"Who, being in very nature God, did not consider equality with God something to be grasped, but made himself nothing, taking the very nature of a servant, being made in human likeness." Phil 2:6f

*"For in Christ all the fullness of the Deity lives in
bodily form."* Col. 2:9

	Dr.	Cr.
Jesus Christ (Humanity)	XXX	
Jesus Christ (Grace)		XXX

The above two journals are just food for thought. The true source of the inexhaustible Credit on the account of Jesus Christ came from His willingness to suffer and die on the cross. On the cross a sinless man becomes sin for all of humanity. The justice quality of God required him to turn his head, as His own son died a slow and painful death.

"My God, my God, why have you forsaken me?"
Matt 27:46

The credit was so significant that it even covered the debits of those who lived and died before the death of Jesus (Heb 10:1-10).

The good news of the gospel is that an accounting transfer is now available to all of humanity. A transfer that removes the debit balance and even results in a reclassification from the regular ledger to the subsidiary ledger called the Book of Life. Those in the book of life are still charged with sin, but if you are listed in the book of life the blood of Jesus Christ continually removes your debit balance.

"But if we walk in the light, as He is in the light, we have fellowship with one another, and the blood of Jesus, his Son, purifies us from all sin." I John 1:7

What does it cost to receive this soul saving transfer? The price is free, if you name Jesus Lord of your life!

*"For it is by grace you have been saved, through
faith - and this is not from yourselves, it is the
gift of God - not by works, so that no one can boast."* Ephesians 2:8

Jesus is our Jubilee. The forgiveness of debt God wanted for His people as outlined in Leviticus 25 was finally fulfilled by Jesus on the cross. (Luke 4:21) Now that is GOOD NEWS!

"The spirit of the Lord is on me, because he has anointed me to preach good news to the poor. He has sent me to proclaim freedom for the prisoners and recovery of sight for the blind, to release the oppressed, and <u>to proclaim the year of the Lord's favor</u>."

ACCOUNTING'S SAINTLY ANCESTRY

By
Dr. Jack E. Bower
Eastern University

Hypothesis: Saint Thomas Aquinas or one of his immediate disciples formulated the system now known as double-entry accounting. This article will show motive and opportunity on the part of this great theologian to address the issue of bookkeeping.

Definition of the Term Double Entry Accounting: Accounting records comprise some of the earliest written documents known to mankind such as the clay tokens found in Mesopotamia that were used as the first bills of lading.[1] Accounting records and reports were developed in the Islamic State beginning in 622 and continued to advance during the development of the Muslim religion.[2] The recording of two sides of a transaction as opposites to one another contains a key element of double entry, but remains a single-entry system until an effort is made to balance the debits against the credits. Most accounting historians accept this definition. The critical question is when did the transition occur from recording two sides of a transaction (single entry) into a self balancing set of accounts (double entry)? There are several theories and as one author has observed: *"Students of the subject, in an endeavor to give due credit for the invention of the system, offer a wide range of possibilities."*[3] This article offers yet another plausible explanation for the invention of double-entry accounting.

Early Accounting Records: For English readers, Professor Geoffrey A. Lee from the University of Nottingham is our renown scholar of ancient accounting documents from this time period. The historical references in this section are from several of his works.[4] The problem is that parchment was scarce and accounting records were seldom preserved. Most accounting historians agree that the oldest known record of the recording of transactions with opposing entries is the Florentine Bank Ledger Fragments of 1211.

In the 1211 ledger there is no effort to balance the accounts of this banking partnership.[5] One theory is that this was a double-entry system, but the balancing portions of the ledger were lost. Another theory is that this ledger combined with other private ledgers being separately maintained would produce a self-balancing set of books.[6] Professor Lee believes that there is strong argument for this hypothesis. Unfortunately, the additional ledgers have never been found to validate this theory.

The oldest surviving record of a valid double-entry accounting system is the ledger of Reniere Fini & Brothers of 1296 to 1305 and the Giovanni Farolfi & Company of 1299 to 1300.[7] Both of these ledgers were self-balancing with a capital account to record the difference between revenue and expense. These accounts show debits and credits in opposition to each other, not simply two parts of the same transaction. The partners' capital account is the algebraic sum of the difference between assets and liabilities. The concept of an accounting period was also starting to develop.[8]

The critical question is what happened between 1211 and 1296? What causes the algebraic breakthrough in bookkeeping? What created the idea of setting things equal to each other? What was the critical intellectual influence of this time period. The answer is quite obvious, Saint Thomas Aquinas lived from about 1225 to 1274.

Economic Context: Medieval society consisted of a feudal economy bound together by tradition. Each estate or kingdom was a complete economic unit capable of supplying all of its physical needs. The lords were given use of the land by the king and they in turn allocated the land to their serfs. The serfs paid the lords in crops or labor and the lords paid the king in crops or money. To not accept the system was rebellion against God.[9] To change the system was opposition to the will of God. But change did take place as technology and other forces began to erode and disrupt the feudal economic system.

The forces of change were addressed by several monks who attempted to prescribe rules of economic conduct compatible with religious doctrine. "The most important of the scholastic writers was St. Thomas Aquinas."[10] The key issue was the ownership of private property. The allocation of scarce resources by price created issues of equity and justice which St. Thomas Aquinas focused upon.[11] Aquinas concluded that making a reasonable profit from a "just price" was not a sin because it was a reasonable means of meeting the needs of the trading parties. The calculation of a "just price" required an accounting system. Aquinas' meeting of human needs was based upon Aristotle's conception of need. In general, Aquinas "advanced economics and all the social sciences by his use of abstract thinking."[12]

"Thomas Aquinas' Summa Theologiae reconciled reason and religion, completed the integration of the classical learning and the Christian theology, and remains to this day the basis of all Catholic theological teaching."[13]

The High Middle Ages: Construction of cities, castles and cathedrals created wealth. Logic and legalism were needed to rule and manage the affairs of men. Accounting for inventory and a fair profit became an issue. Max Weber believed that "the development of double-entry book-keeping".. "was a phenomenon of major importance in opening the way for the regularizing of capitalistic enterprise."[14]

In general, a spirit of optimism and self-satisfaction was widespread, encouraged by rising material prosperity. Of course, prosperity was metal kitchenware and candles for the poor. For the rich, prosperity was fine wall hangings and bed furnishings or chests with hinges and locks. The wealthy could even afford windows of glass in their homes.[15] It is hard for people in modern societies to appreciate the desperate need for reason and logic in the Middle Ages. Superstitions ruled the day. For example, relics such as bones were of extreme importance. The bones of famous persons were a major commodity of exchange and some feared that they were more valuable dead, as bones, than alive. When Saint Thomas Aquinas died his body was decapitated and boiled in the monastery of Fossanuova in order to keep his bones.[16] Logic and reason were scarce commodities and St. Thomas Aquinas was the major provider of a voice of reason during these transitional times.

The Education of St. Thomas Aquinas: Dominic of Caleruega in

Spain was a devoted friend and ally of Saint Francis. He was a scholar and an excellent administrator. His goal was a higher academy in the greater monasteries and a kind of graduate school in the major cities. He established a school in Paris in 1220. The Paris school together with the one in Oxford became the intellectual centers of the West.[17] Saint Thomas attended the school in Paris.

The intellectual battle of the high Middle Ages was in two camps. One school of thought was led by Saint Bernard of Clairvaux (Franciscans). Bernard said you can find more in forests than in books, although he praised poetry. He represented the distrust of science and reason. He tried to bring Peter Abelard, the intellectual leader of the other camp (the Dominicans & Scholasticism), to trial for heresy. Eventually, the camp of reason won the day and the writings of St. Thomas Aquinas were widely accepted. Scholasticism is essentially the application of reason to revelation. It accepts the words of Scripture without question, but clarifies them by reason. Aquinas was a modern realist. Reason was God's gift to mankind and must necessarily confirm the truths of the faith. If it does not, than something has gone astray.[18]

Saint Thomas Aquinas was not without his critics: *"Scholasticism put an end to the confusion of philosophy with poetry, rhetoric, proverbial lore, and the various learning of the schools. The old connection between artes and philosophy is severed at a blow."*[19] So writes Ernst Curtius as he reflects on the decline of poetry and literature under the Scholastics, particularly under the writings of St. Thomas Aquinas. Other writers, like Brewer, are very critical of the Scholasticism, because it was far too pragmatic and rational. He calls St. Thomas Aquinas a "boy" who knows nothing of the world. Even major literary collections such as The World in Literature will acknowledge the impact of St. Thomas Aquinas on reason and attitudes of the high Middle Ages, but do not consider his works to be literary classics.[20]

Proportionality and the influence of Holy Scripture: The first to promulgate generally accepted accounting principles (GAAP) was Pacioli.[21] His book was titled Summa de Arithmethica, Geometria, Proportioni et Proportionality, and was first published in 1494, about two hundred years after the earliest record of double entry accounting.[22] Pacioli does not claim to have invented the system, and does not give any indication of the original author other than it is the method of Venice (chapter one). The writings of Pacioli are full of references to scripture and to the providence of God. He says that every journal page is to have the name of God (Sweet Jesus) at the top or at a minimum the cross of Christ. According to Pacioli, the use of God's name on every page is a generally accepted accounting principle. Near the end of the book, in chapter 34, he asks the readers to "pray to God for me that I may proceed by always doing well to His praise and glory." When he mentions the closing of the profit and loss account, he says, *"If the loss exceeds the profit, may God protect each of us who is really a good Christian from such a state of affairs, then credit the account in the usual manner."* Making a profit is good, in the beginning of his book he says: *"The end or objective of every businessman is to make a lawful and satisfactory profit so that he may remain in business."* [23]

Two issues can be observed from the first author of accounting: #1 the term proportionate was a part of the title of the mathematics text that included the section on double-entry accounting and #2 the accounting system was directly linked to the spiritual writings of the clergy. If Saint Thomas was the major influence on the development of double-entry accounting, then the references to the providence's of God and the concern for a just profit are entirely appropriate. If, on the other hand, the first accounting system did not develop within the clergy then the scriptural references that were considered the standards of the time, seem strangely misplaced just as they would today. The significance of the endorsement to permit the making of a profit by merchants, first argued by Saint Thomas Aquinas, should not be underestimated. His motive for influencing the development of an accounting system would be the control of a "just profit." The same theme was woven into the writings of Pacioli as he tried to promulgate this spiritually integrated accounting system.

The use of the label **proportionate** is also significant. The Greek word from which we get the English word proportionate is "analogos".[24] An analogy is the correspondence between things otherwise dissimilar.[25] What is a journal entry but an analogy? The early authors of accounting perceived the journal entry as the critical part of the system, the book of original entry. Pacioli went into great detail to illustrate each type of journal entry using double lines to separate the "per" and the "a." (He preferred these to debits and credits). How does the use of analogy connect with Saint Thomas Aquinas? Scholars of his work refer to him as the father of the analogy. Many scholars say that this is what he is best known for.[26] The last point deserves a note of caution. The analogy for which Saint Thomas Aquinas was famous, was a "logical doctrine about the meaning of words."[27] He would not have used the equal sign in his construction of an analogy. They also did not use negative number during this time period, hence the need for debits and credits. Saint Thomas Aquinas was not a mathematical person but, he loved to connect things together.

"Aristotelian theory of cause and effect was applied to everyday life and to the nature of God by Saint Thomas Aquinas."[28] What is a journal entry but the recording of everyday events with a cause and effect. Is it a powerful argument for connectivity that the life of the person who advanced the theory of the analogy and logic coincides exactly with the development of double-entry accounting? As one scholar has noted, it was actually the disciples of Saint Thomas Aquinas that turned his theory into methods (methods such as "proportioni et Proportionalita"): *"The philosophical activity of the master became doctrine in the hands of his disciples. Constructing a theory turned analogy into method and gave the discussion a particular turn: does it work?"*[29]

The invention of movable metal type in 1454 should also not be underestimated.[30] If Saint Thomas Aquinas or his disciples did in fact conceive the first double-entry accounting system that became known as the method of Venice, the printing press was not available to disseminate the information. When the press was available for use, other than for making Bibles, it was used by Pacioli. It is also interesting to note that subsequent accounting authors such as Manzoni said the same things as the <u>Summa</u> without giving credit to Pacioli.[31] This is further evidence that some lost manuscript by Saint Thomas Aquinas on Proportioni et Proportionalita was available to the early authors of books on mathematics.

Conclusion: The dominant theory on the origin of double-entry accounting is that it is "neither a discovery of science nor the inspiration of a happy moment, but the outcome of continued efforts to meet the changing necessities of trade."[32] The method of Venice is attributed to the merchants and bankers of Florence, Venice and Genoa during the thirteenth century.[33] Could a system such as double entry evolve over time? Possibly, but it has not changed dramatically in the last 500 years. The text written by Pacioli could still be used in a principles of accounting classroom today. Did it take the brilliance of a person such as Saint Thomas Aquinas to provide the missing ingredients of self balancing accounts?

The life of the father of the analogy living and teaching at the same time that proportionality was considered a part of the study of mathematics and bookkeeping is difficult to accept as coincidence. Note that Saint Thomas Aquinas was a practical and technical writer, not a poet or literature great. He was an Italian monk with an intense concern for a just price which gave him every reason to address the accounting issue, his writings are full of economic issues. Would the merchants of Venice have integrated spiritual principles into the accounting system? It seems highly unlikely.

Saint Thomas Aquinas was the dominant intellectual figure of that time period, and the purpose and intent of his work coincides perfectly with the development of double-entry accounting. The rationale for the connection between the two is obvious. Perhaps, someday a manuscript will be discovered to prove or disprove this hypothesis. Until then, it makes a great topic for discussion and further research.

Bibliography

Abacus, December, 1973

Aquinas, Thomas. <u>Summa Theological.</u>

Bauers, Walter. Arndt and Gingrich, <u>Greek-English</u>
<u>Lexicon of the New Testament and</u> <u>Other Early Christian</u>
<u>Literature.</u> University of Chicago Press, 1877-1960.

Brown, Richard ed. <u>A History of Accounting and</u>
<u>Accountants.</u> Augustus M Kelly Publishing, N.Y. 1968.

Burrell, David. <u>Aquinas.</u> U. of Notre Dame Press, 1979.

Curtius, Ernst Robert. Translated by Willard Trask.
<u>European Literature and the Latin Middle Ages.</u> Harper &
Row, N.Y. 1953.

Geijsbeck, John. <u>Ancient Double Entry Bookkeeping.</u>
Scholars Books Co. Houston,   Texas, 1914.

Giddens, Anthony. Introduction to *"The Protestant Ethic*
and the Spirit of Capitalism by Max Weber" Charles
Scribner's Sons, New York, 1958.

Journal of Accounting Research. Spring 1973.

Kenny, Anthony. <u>The Five Ways of St. Thomas Aquinas'</u>
<u>Proofs of God's Existence.</u>   University of Notre Dame Press,
1969.

Kotker, Norman. Editor. Morris Bishop author. <u>Middle</u>
<u> Ages.</u> American Heritage Pub. Co. Inc., 1968.

Landreth, Harry & Colander, David. <u>History of</u>
<u> Economic Thought.</u> Houghton Mifflin   Company,

Princeton, N.J., 1994.

Langer, William. Editor. An Encyclopedia of World
        History. 4th. Edition, Houghton Mifflin Company, Boston,
        1968.

Lee, Geoffrey A. *Abacus.* December, 1979.

Lee, Geoffrey A. The coming of age of double entry:
        The Giovanni Farolfi Ledger of 1299-1300. The Accounting
        Historians Journal, Fall 1977.

Lee, Geoffrey A. The Florentine Bank Ledger Fragments
        of 1211, Journal of Accounting Research, Spring 1973.

Littleton, A.C. Accounting Evolution to 1900. U. of
        Alabama Press, The Academy of Accounting Historians,
        1981.

Nottingham Medieval Studies, Vol XVI. 1972.

Pergallo, Edward. Origin and Evolution of Double Enty
        Bookkeeping, A Study of Italian Practice from the Fourteenth
        Century. American Institute Publishing Company,   1939.

The Roots of Writing. Time. August 1, 1977, page 76.

Warnock, Robert & Anderson, George. The World in
        Literature. Scott, Foresman and Co. Two Vols. The Ancient
        Foundations & Centuries of Transition. 1967.

Zaid, Omar Abdullah. *"The Accounting Historians Journal."* Vol.
        27, No. 1, June 2000. by Birmingham Printing and Pub. Co. Al. 2000

[1] *"The Roots of Writing,"* Time, August 1, 1977, page 76.

[2] Zaid, Omar Abdullah. *"Were Islamic Records Precursors to Accounting Books
Based on the Italian Method?"* Accounting Historians Journal, Vol 27, No. 1, June
2000. page 87.

[3] Edward Pergallo, <u>Origin and Evolution of Double Entry Bookkeeping, A Study of Italian Practice from the Fourteenth Century</u>, American Institute Publishing Company, 1939, page 1.

[4] *Journal of Accounting Research*, Spring 1973, 47-61 & *Abacus,* December 1973, 137-155 & *Nottingham Medieval Studies*, Vol XVI, 1972, pages 28-60.

[5] Geoffrey A. Lee, <u>The Florentine Bank Ledger Fragments of 1211,</u> Journal of Accounting Research, Spring 1973, page 47-61.

[6] Geoffrey Lee, <u>Abacus,</u> December 1979, pages 148ff.

[7] Some historians argue that the ledger of the "Massari of the Commune of Genoa" dated 1340 is the first complete example of a double entry accounting system. See: Edward Peragallo, <u>Origins and evolution of double entry bookkeeping,</u> 1938, page 3.

[8] Geoffrey A. Lee, <u>The coming of age of double entry: The Giovanni Farolfi ledger of 1299-1300,</u> The Accounting Historians Journal, Fall 1977, page 51.

[9] "Everyone must submit himself to the governing authorities, for there is no authority except that which God has established. The authorities that exist have been established by God. Consequently, he who rebels against the authority is rebelling against what God has instituted, and those who do so will bring judgment on themselves." Romans 13:1-2 NIV translation.

[10] Harry Landreth & David Colander, <u>History of Economic Thought</u>, Houghton Mifflin Company, Princeton N.J. 1994, page 30.

[11] William Benton, Publisher, Biographical Note, St. Thomas Aquinas, <u>The Summa Theologica</u>, Vol I, Encyclopedia Britannica, Inc., 1952. "Thomas between 1265 and 1269 commented on the Physics, Metaphysics, On the Soul, Ethics, Politics, and the Posterior Analytics." page vi.

[12] Harry Landreth & David Colander,<u> History of Economic Thought</u>, page 32.

[13] William Langer, Editor; <u>An Encyclopedia of World History,</u> 4th Edition, Houghton Mifflin Company, Boston, 1968, page 247.

[14] Giddens, Anthony. Introduction to "The Protestant Ethic and the Spirit of Capitalism" by Max Weber, page 8.

[15] Norman Kotker editor, Morris Bishop author, <u>Middle Ages</u>, American Heritage Pub. Co. Inc. 1968, page 37.

[16] Ibid., page 131.

[17] Ibid., page 154.

[18] Ibid., page 274.

[19] Ernst Robert Curtius, translated by Willard Trask, <u>European Literature and the Latin Middle Ages,</u> published by Harper & Row N.Y. 1953, page 213.

[20] Robert Warnock and George Anderson, <u>The World in Literature,</u> published by Scott, Foresman and Co. two vol. <u>The Ancient Foundations</u> & <u>Centuries of Transition</u>, 1967.

[21] There is considerable dispute over the name Pacioli as it was translated. Some scholars prefer Paciolo. The name used for some of the later books was Fra. Paciolo di Borgo Santo Sepolcro. In certain books his name is Patiolus.

[22] John Geijsbeck, Ancient Double-Entry Bookkeeping, Scholars Book Co. Houston Texas, 1914. The best collections of the works of Paciloli are at the Geijsbeck-Lawrence Library in Denver and at Harvard University Library, Cambridge, Mass. The second printing of the Summa was in 1523.

[23] There are two translations of the Summa into English. The most accurate was by Pietro Crivelli, but the most readable was by John B. Geijsbeek. Most scholars prefer the translation by Geijsbeek as illustrated above.

[24] Walter Bauer's, Arndt and Gingrich, Greek-English Lexicon of the New Testament and Other Early Christian Literature, University of Chicago Press, 1877-1960, page 57, "right relationship, proportion.. in right relationship to..in agreement with..or in proportion to .."

[25] The American Heritage Dictionary, second college edition, Houghton Mifflin Co. Boston, page 106.

[26] David B. Burrell, Aquinas, University of Notre Dame Press, 1979, page 55. David Burrell tries to argue that historians have taken the grammatical astuteness of Aquinas as a replacement for his intuition. This is interesting to David Burrell because he says "it should direct us to his practice instead of to his theory". Double-entry accounting may have been one of the practices of St. Thomas Aquinas.

[27] Therese Bonin, a well published scholar on St. Thomas Aquinas, commenting on this chapter and the theory that Saint Thomas Aquinas used algebraic logic.

[28] Anthony Kenny, The Five Ways of St. Thomas Aquinas' Proofs of God's Existence, University of Notre Dame Press, 1969. (An excellent book on the formulations of St. Thomas Aquinas).

[29] David Burrell, Aquinas, U. of Notre Dame Press, 1979, page 55.

[30] This is the traditional date for the invention of printing from movable metal type. Usually attributed to Johann Gutenberg who lived from 1398 to 1468.

[31] There are about 50 books on accounting written between 1494 (Pacioli) and 1636 (the English book on the keeping of accounts "after the Italian manner").

[32] Richard Brown, ed. A History of Accounting and Accountants, Augustus M. Kelly Publishing, N.Y. 1968, page 93.

[33] Ibid. page 99.

Part III

Supplemental Lecture Material

'COUNTING IN THE GLOBAL VILLAGE

[handwritten: more complex BUT ALLOWS FOR MORE LOOP HOLES. FOReign COUNTRIES ARE MORE simple & BASIC]

By
Dr. Jack E. Bower
Eastern University

We have become a global village. Respect for people from other backgrounds and empathy towards those of diverse faith and culture as become a basic professional competence in the 21ˢᵗ century. Competition for many industries is now defined globally. Trading in cross-boarder financial markets has become commonplace and discipline of accounting is rapidly becoming globally conceptualized. *"Love your neighbor as your self"* is a universal principle. International trade and competition achieved significant progress in the economic development of third world nations. Overall the standard of living continues to rise worldwide as a result of international trade as well as many positive changes in international policy environment. Financial information is the transmission element that makes trade possible. The role of international accounting standards in the global village is vital.

The International Accounting Standards Board (IASB) is an independent decision making body established in January 2001, similar in structure to the Financial Accounting Standards Board (FASB), which serves the same functions for the United States. The new structure was the recommendation of the "Strategy Working Party," established in 1997 by the International Accounting Standards Committee, the predecessor of the IASB.[1] The goal of the IASB is to promote uniformity in accounting principles around the world.[2] The United States has the world's largest economy and the most extensive and well-developed collection of Generally Accepted Accounting Principles (GAAP). As of the summer of 2002, there are 145 FASB Statements of Financial Accounting Standards (SFAS), 7 Financial Accounting Concepts, 43 Interpretations and 97 Technical Bulletins. This significant collection of accounting literature continues to have a major impact on the development of IASB principles. Generally Accepted Accounting Principles and International Accounting Principles are very similar and continue to move towards mutual harmony.[3]

Here is an example of the standard setting process. On April 21, 1999 the FASB voted to rule out the Pooling of Interest Method of accounting for business combinations forcing the use of the purchases method, which creates goodwill. This was a significant move towards harmonization. The Wall Street business community in the U.S. complained about the FASB ruling to Congress, and after much debate, it was vetoed by the S.E.C. In the summer of 2001, the FASB issued SFAS 142, to no longer require the amortization (expensing) of goodwill created by the purchases method (the expensing of goodwill was lowering projected earnings from mergers). This removed the objection to the use of the purchases method by corporations wanting to merge. In the end, everyone got what they wanted and the U.S. is now very close to IAS 22 & 40 which requires fair value reporting. Now the decrease in the value of goodwill is an audit issue for public accountants to address each year. The point is that we are moving towards a more unified set of accounting standards! Are we there yet?[4] No, but in cases where they are not similar, the U.S. method is generally permitted. For example, the Last In First Out (LIFO) method of inventory valuation is U.S. GAAP and permitted by international standards. The other 103 countries that belong to the IASB almost universally reject it.

International Accounting Standards, when viewed from a U.S. perspective appear less complicated and less complex than U.S. GAAP. IASB principles are designed to provide the minimum amount of guidance. This also means that a significant amount of double accounting treatments are permissible. The IASB Board refers to the preferred method as a "benchmark" so as not to offend the country using the less preferred method.

For more information contact:
International Accounting Standards Board
    30 Cannon Street, London EC4M 6XH,
    United Kingdom
    Telephone: +44 (0)20 7246 6410
    Facsimile: +44 (0)20 7246 6411
    Publications Facsimile: +44 (0)20 7353 0562
    E-mail: iasb@iasb.org.uk

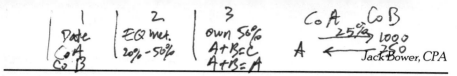

The following list and brief comparison provides a framework for discussion of International Accounting Standards and U.S. GAAP. 2003

IAS 1 – Presentation of Financial Statements – defines the overall considerations for the basic four financial statements; fair presentation, accounting policies, going concern, accrual basis of accounting, consistency, materiality and aggregation, offsetting and comparative information. The standard prescribes the minimum structure and content including certain information required on the face of the financial statements.

This is similar in coverage to the six Statements of Financial Accounting Concepts (SFAC) with some notable exceptions such as the lack of the requirement for the distinction of current/noncurrent assets in the Balance Sheet.

IAS 2 – Inventories – Lower of cost (which include costs to bring the inventories to their present condition and location) or net realizable value. If cost cannot be determined, then LIFO (with disclosure requirements) or weighted average formulas are permitted.

The permitting of the LIFO method is a concession to the U.S. Similar to L.C.M. in the U.S. APB 43

IAS 3 – Consolidated Financial Statements – Superseded by IAS 27 (1989) and IAS 28 (1989).

IAS 4 – Depreciation Accounting – Superseded by IAS 16 with respect to depreciation of property, plant and equipment. Superseded by IAS 38, with respect to amortization of intangible assets. Withdrawn.

IAS 5 - Information to be Disclosed in Financial Statements – Superseded by IAS 1.

IAS 6 - Accounting Responses to Changing Prices – Superseded by IAS 15.

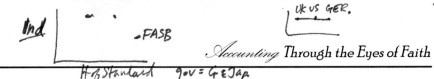

IAS 7 – Cash Flow Statements – Cash flow statement is divided into operating, investing, and financial activities. Direct or Indirect method is permitted.

The same format as the U.S. FASB No. 95 (1987) but with more detail and disclosure in the footnotes.

IAS 8 – Net Profit or Loss for the Period, Fundamental Errors and Changes in Accounting Policies – Separate disclosure in the notes is required for extraordinary items and ordinary but abnormal items of income and expense. Changes in accounting estimates are reflected prospectively. Correction of an error is treated as a prior period adjustment and a change in accounting policy is treated retrospectively by restating all prior periods presented.

This is similar to APB Opinion 9, 26, & 30 on extraordinary items and SFAS 4 on extinguishment of debt as extraordinary.

IAS 9 – Research and Development Costs – Superseded by IAS 38.

IAS 10 – Events After the Balance Sheet Date – Financial statements should be adjusted for events occurring after the Balance Sheet date that provide further evidence of conditions present before the Balance Sheet date. New information discovered before the issuance of the financial statements on conditions present before the Balance Sheet date should be disclosed in the financial statements. Financial statements should not be adjusted for events occurring after the Balance Sheet date that reflect on conditions occurring after the Balance Sheet date.

This is similar to US AICPA GAAS Section 560.03 to .09 but the IAS language is stronger.

IAS 11 – Construction Contracts – "Percentage of completion method" should be used if the contract price, past and future costs, and percentage of completion are known or can be reasonably estimated. If not, the "cost recovery method" should be used (costs are expensed and revenues are recognized to the extent of costs expensed). In both cases, expected losses should be recognized immediately. The "cost recovery method" varies from the "completed contract method" in that with the "completed contract method", no profits are recognized until the completion of the project.

This is similar to US GAAP (Accounting Research Bulletin 45, AICPA SOP 81-1, & APB 10).

IAS 12 – Income Taxes – Accrue for deferred tax liabilities for taxable temporary differences. Accrue for deferred tax assets for deductible temporary differences only if it is probable a tax benefit will be realized.

This is similar to SFAS 109 with a stronger emphasis on "reasonable expectation of realization" for the balance in the deferred taxes payable account.

IAS 13 – Presentation of Current Assets and Current Liabilities – Superseded by IAS 1.

IAS 14 – Segment Reporting – Segment information by geographical area is required. If consolidated financial statements are presented, the segment reporting is also consolidated. There are two bases for segmentation (primary and secondary), each with different disclosure requirements.

This is similar to SFAS 14.

IAS 15 – Information Reflecting the Effects of Changing Prices – Encouraged but not required unless required in the country of domicile. Current Cost Approach and Purchasing Power Approach are acceptable but there is no international consensus on the subject.

This was formerly a US requirement under SFAS 33, but was eliminated by SFAS 82.

IAS 16 – Property, Plant and Equipment – Initial measurement should be at cost, then depreciate. An alternative is to use the fair value approach. If the fair value approach is used, it should be used for all like assets. Unlike US GAAP, even under the depreciation cost method, revaluation is allowed.

Under US GAAP, the fair value approach is not allowed for Property, Plant and Equipment except as unaudited supplementary information.

IAS 17 – Leases – Substance of the transaction over form of the contract. A finance lease (capital lease under US GAAP) is defined as one that transfers substantially all the risks and rewards to the lessee. A finance lease should be capitalized at the lower of fair value or the present value of lease payments. Operating leases are treated as current operating expenses.

This is similar to SFAS 13.

IAS 18 – Revenue – Essential criterion for the recognition of revenue.

This is similar to APB Opinion 10 & FAC 5.

IAS 19 – Employee Benefits – Defined contribution plans are a trust account. Defined benefit plans require the use of actuarial principles.

A table is available on the IASC web site (www.iasc.org.uk) that illustrates the differences between IAS 19 and US GAAP.

IAS 20 – Accounting for Government Grants and Disclosure of Government Assistance – "Grants should not be credited directly to equity, but recognized as income in a way matched with related costs. Grants related to assets should be deducted from the cost or treated as deferred income."

Deferred revenue is acceptable U.S. G.A.A.P., APB No. 29 & FASB EITF 86-29, but the recording grants as contra asset accounts are not.

IAS 21 – The Effects of Changes in Foreign Exchange Rates – (Translation into one reporting entity, not between countries for the convenience of readers.) Transactions are recorded at the exchange rate on the transaction date. Differences between the recorded amount and the settlement amount are a gain or loss. Proper accruals should be made at year-end. Integral part of operations of the parent – effect of the exchange rate change has an immediate impact on the monetary items held by the parent rather than just the parent's net investment in the operation (not an integral part). The translation of the foreign financial statements into those of the parent should achieve the same effect as if all transactions of the foreign operation had been entered into by the parent.

SFAS 52 recognizes the gain or loss between transaction date and settlement date. No standards for "integral part of operations." The IAS is more involved than the US standard.

IAS 22 – Business Combinations – The Purchase Method is to be used in most cases with the Pooling of Interests Method only to be used when nether party is identified as the acquirer. Goodwill is defined as the difference between the purchase price and the fair value of the net assets.

SFAS 141, which supersedes APB Opinion 16, requires business combinations to be accounted for using the purchase method. The Pooling of Interest Method was removed from US GAAP to provide more international harmonization. In addition, SFAS 142, which supersedes APB Opinion 17, eliminates the amortization of goodwill and requires an annual test for impairment instead. This is very different than the IAS, which does not permit an enterprise to assign an infinite life to goodwill and still requires the amortization method. The IAS requires annual testing for impairment, when the useful life of the goodwill is estimated to be more than 20 years.

IAS 23 – Borrowing Costs - Capitalization of borrowing costs is not required. These requirements are "set out" if the enterprise elects to follow the capitalization approach. This follows the US standard of SFAS 34 including the "not to exceed actual" requirement. US standard is more complex and specific.

IAS 24 – Related Party Disclosures – Similar standards as SFAS 57.

IAS 25 – Accounting for Investments - Superseded by IAS 39 and IAS 40.

IAS 26 – Accounting and Reporting by Retirement Benefit Plans – This standard complements IAS 19. Applicable to insurance companies and any separate legal entity that is a trust for pension benefits. It simply defines the report contents for retirement benefit plans.

This is similar to AICPA Industry audit guides for the insurance industry. In the US, these types of organizations are a special type of nonprofit corporation.

IAS 27 – Consolidated Financial Statements and Accounting for Investments in Subsidiaries – The standard provides the framework for intercompany eliminations (intragroup eliminations). The word "subsidiary" is defined as an investment, where the power of control is exercised, but not necessarily over 50% control. If the investment "subsidiary" is covered under IAS 39 and IAS 40, then it is an investment and not part of the consolidated financial statements. Also, subsidiaries that are accounted for by the equity method under IAS 28 are not part of the consolidated financial statements.

Similar to U.S. FASB No. 115. The permitting of the equity method here and in IAS 28 is another concession to the U.S. The equity method is unique to the U.S. and considered illogical to most international accounting bodies.

IAS 28 – Accounting for Investments in Associates – Associate is defined as an enterprise in which the investor has significant influence. Both the Cost and Equity Method are permitted. Guidance is given as to which method would be appropriate.

IAS 29 – Financial Reporting in Hyperinflationary Economies – Balance Sheet amounts not already expressed as in terms of the monetary unit current at the Balance Sheet date are restated by applying a general price index. If a general price index is not available, use the movement in exchange rate between the reporting currency and a relatively stable foreign currency. Never exceed the recoverable amount (market value) of any restated items. Do not use IAS 21 when restating Balance Sheet accounts. Differences are credited to the "revaluation surplus" account. All movements are to be disclosed under IAS 5 including the basis for the restatement. Income statement amounts should also be restated by applying a general price index. Corresponding figures for previous reporting periods and consolidated financial statements are to be restated using the general price index approach.

Not fully a part of US GAAP or GAAS but the U.S. is moving in that direction. SFAS 107 Disclosure about Fair Value of Financial Instruments and the host of pronouncements on impairment such as SFAS 118, 121 & 137. SFAS 142, Goodwill and Other Intangibles also moved the U.S. closer to fair value accounting.

IAS 30 – Disclosures in the Financial Statements of Banks and Similar Financial Institutions – (See AICPA "Audit Guide for Banks".) Harmonization of the different methods of bank reporting and measurement or items in the financial statements is beyond the scope of this statement. This statement is simply a list of disclosures necessary for compliance with IAS.

IAS 31 – Financial Reporting of Interests in Joint Ventures – Jointly controlled operations – separate accounting records for the joint venture are not required.

Jointly controlled assets – separate accounting records are not required but if presented must be limited to the expenses incurred in common by the ventures and ultimately borne by the venturers according to their agreed shares.

Jointly controlled entities – application of "proportionate consolidation" only the venturer's share of the joint venture is reported in the consolidated financial statements. Separate financial statements are prepared in order to meet a variety of needs with the result that different reporting practices are in use in different countries. This statement does not indicate a preface for any particular treatment.

This is similar to US GAAP; Proportionate Share Accounting, APB Opinion 18 (Joint Venture = Partnership).

IAS 32 – Financial Instruments: Disclosure and Presentation – classification reflects substance, not form. What is debt - mandatorily redeemable preferred stock is debt and deduction of interest on the income statement. IAS 39 requires certain disclosures.

This is similar to SFAS 129 and SEC Accounting Rules, sec. 211.01 & 211.04. Note; substance over form is basic US business law

IAS 33 – Earnings Per Share – public companies only, must disclose basic and diluted net income on the face of the statement, and for each class of stock.

This is similar to APB Opinion 15 and SFAS 128 on Earnings Per Share.

IAS 34 – Interim Financial Reporting – contains both presentation and measurement guidance, defines the minimum content of an interim report, and sets out the accounting recognition and measurement principles to be followed in any interim financial statement.

This is similar to APB Opinion 28, which was clarified by SFAS 131.

IAS 35 – Discontinuing Operations – focuses on how to present discontinued operations in an enterprise's financial statements and what information to disclose. It does not establish any new principles for deciding when and how to recognize and measure income, expense, cash flows and charges in assets and liabilities relating to a discontinued operation.

This is similar to APB Opinion 30 as explained by the 1973 AICPA report, "Reporting the Results of Operations."

IAS 36 – Impairment of Assets – deals with accounting for impairment of goodwill, intangible assets and property, plant and equipment. The standard includes requirements for identifying an impaired asset, measuring its recoverable amount, recognizing or reversing any resulting impairment loss, and disclosing information on impairment losses or reversals of impairment losses.

This is similar to SFAS 121. IAS 36 and SFAS 121 both use present value calculations to find the value of the asset.

IAS 37 – Provisions, Contingent Liabilities and Contingent Assets – provisions should be recognized in the Balance Sheet when an enterprise has a present obligation as a result of a past event. The Statement uses the terms "probable" and "remote" as determining factors.

This is similar to SFAS 5 and Interpretation 34, but this IAS does not address obligations that are callable by the creditor, SFAS 78.

IAS 38 – Intangible Assets – applies to advertising, training, start-up and R&D costs.

This is similar to SFAS 2, which states that enterprises must disclose all R&D expenses and APB Opinion 17, which states that enterprises must disclose the method of amortization. Under IAS, the items acquired for a particular research project that have no alternative future uses are expensed as items are used in the project. In contrast, such costs are expensed when incurred under GAAP in the US, Germany, and Mexico. Capitalization of R&D expenses occurs in Brazil and Japan. In Canada and the United Kingdom, the research costs are expensed and the development costs are capitalized.

IAS 39 – Financial Instruments: Recognition and Measurement – Subsequent to initial recognition, all financial assets are remeasured to fair value, except those not held for trading or not held to maturity or whose fair value can not be readily measured.

This is similar to SFAS 115 and SFAS 133. The fair value of the hedge and accounting for the hedge depends on the type of hedge. A table comparing the IAS and US GAAP is available at the IASC web site (www.iasc.org.uk).

IAS 40 – Investment Property - is not limited to enterprises whose main activities are in this area. Investment property is property (land or a building - or part of a building - or both) held (by the owner or by the lessee under a finance lease) to earn rentals or for capital appreciation or both. Investment property does not include property held as inventory, property under construction, finance lease (capital lease under US GAAP), regenerative natural resources and mineral rights. Under IAS 40, an enterprise must choose either the fair value model (investment property should be measured at fair value and changes in fair value should be recognized in the income statement); or the cost model (investment property should be measured at depreciated cost less any accumulated impairment losses). An enterprise that chooses the cost model should disclose the fair value of its investment property. IAS 40 also requires consistency in applying the chosen method to all investment property and discourages a change from one model to the other.

The U.S. is not ready to move to complete fair value accounting. The U.S. is however making progress in this direction. SFAS 142 is a good example, requiring the annual evaluation of the fair value of goodwill. SFAS 107 also requires market value accounting for investments which is very close to the international standard.

IAS 41 – Agriculture (effective 1/1/2003) – prescribes the accounting treatment, financial statement presentation and disclosures related to agricultural activity. Biological assets and agricultural produce harvested from the biological assets should be measured at their fair value less estimated point-of-sale costs, except where fair value cannot be measured reliably. After the point of harvest, IAS 2 (Inventories) should be applied. The standard allows for biological assets to be measured at cost less any accumulated depreciation and any accumulated impairment losses if fair value is not reliably measurable. Enterprise must disclose reasons for this valuation.

This is not similar to U.S. GAAP. However, SFAS 40 Financial Reporting and Changing Prices: Specialized Assets, addresses the same issues from a U.S. perspective.

---

[1] FASB description of the IASB "The new structure has characteristics similar to that of the FASB's   structure. There is an IASC Board of Trustees, an independent, mostly full-time standard setting Board called the IASB, and an

Advisory Council. The IASB held its first meeting to discuss technical issues in April 2001. Like the FASB, IASB meetings to discuss technical issues are open to the public." http://www.fasb.org/IASC/iasb.shtml

2 IASB Constitution "The objectives of IASC are: (a) to develop, in the public interest, a single set of high quality, understandable and enforceable global accounting standards that require high quality, transparent and comparable information in financial statements and other financial reporting to help participants in the world's capital markets and other users make economic decisions; (b) to promote the use and rigorous application of those standards; and (c) to bring about convergence of national accounting standards and International Accounting Standards to high quality solutions." http://www.iasc.org.

3 FASB description of the differences between U.S. GAAP and International Standards "The FASB's obligation to its domestic constituents demands that it attempt to narrow the range of difference between the U.S. and   other countries' standards. High-quality financial information is essential to analysis and assessment of investment opportunities to ensure the efficient allocation of capital both within and across national borders." http://www.fasb.org/IASC/

4 FASB view of the need for harmonization "Ideally, international analysts and investors would like to compare   financial statements (both domestic and foreign) based on the same accounting standards, especially if those standards raise the overall quality of financial information. At present, a single set of high-quality international accounting standards that is accepted in all capital markets does not exist. In the United States, for example,   domestic firms that are registrants with the Securities and Exchange Commission (SEC) must file financial reports using U.S. generally accepted accounting principles (GAAP). Foreign firms filing with the SEC can use U.S. GAAP, their home country GAAP, or international standards—although if they use their home country   GAAP or international standards, foreign issuers must provide a reconciliation to U.S. GAAP." http://www.fasb.org/IASC/

"PAY CAESAR WHAT BELONGS TO CAESAR"[1]

No More and No Less

By
Dr. Jack E. Bower
Eastern University

WHAT IS THE DIFFERENCE.

Introduction

Accountants should practice tax avoidance, not tax evasion. Paying government agencies the proper amount and no more, fulfills the teaching of our Lord Jesus Christ and allows for a proper amount to be committed to God's activities. Giving more to Caesar than what Caesar deserves means less is available for God's purposes. The Apostle Paul confirmed this perspective of obedience in his letter to the Roman, chapter 13:

> *"Everyone is to obey the governing authorities, because there is no authority except from God and so whatever authorities exist have been appointed by God. So anyone who disobeys and authority is rebelling against God's ordinance; and rebels must expect to receive the condemnation they deserve. Magistrates bring fear not to those who do good, but to those who do evil. So if you want to live with no fear of authority, live honestly and you will have its approval; it is there to serve God for you and for your good. But if you do what is wrong, then you may well be afraid; because it is not for nothing that the symbol of authority is the sword; it is there to serve God too, as his avenger, to bring retribution to wrongdoers. You must be obedient therefore, not only because of this retribution, but also for conscience's sake. And this is why you should pay taxes; too,*

because the authorities are all serving God as his agents, even while they are busily occupied with that particular task. Pay to each one what is due to each; taxes to the one to whom tax is due, tolls to the one to whom tolls are due, respect to the one to who respect is due, honour to the one to who honour is due."[2]

    Determining the proper amount due to the Internal Revenue Service (IRS) can be an extremely complex matter. The shear volume of Internal Revenue Code, Regulations, Tax Cases and IRS publications is overwhelming without proper guidance. The purpose of the chapter is to provide the **research essentials** necessary to navigate our complex federal tax environment so that we can be *trustworthy in handling worldly wealth*[3] This knowledge is critical for the accountants of Christian ministries desiring to have IRS nonprofit status. After reading this chapter you should be ready to begin a topical study on a manual or electronic system. Learning to do tax research can help you lower your taxes and also provide some intellectual satisfaction.

    Tax research requires time, patience and the proper resource materials. Obviously, accountants who practice in the U.S. must have a working knowledge of the Internal Revenue Code (IRC) in order to be an effective tax practitioner. A storehouse of tax research material is available to U.S. accountants at public libraries, university libraries over the web and of course, many accountants develop their own rather extensive libraries. The most widely used source for tax research books in the U.S. is Commerce Clearing House (CCH), Inc., 4025 West Peterson Aye, Chicago, Illinois 60646. The U.S. government (IRS) also uses CCH for its copies of the Code. Much of the material presented in this chapter is public information from C.C.H. publications. Several law schools have the entire U.S. Code, including the IRC (title 26), on the Internet. Some individuals also maintain the IRC and other useful tax information on the Internet. Unfortunately, the IRS does not maintain the Code and Regulations on the Net. They are available, however, as a part of the Federal Register on the site of the National Archives & Record Administration:

http://www.archives.gov/federal_register/index.html

Understanding the Outline of the Internal Revenue Code
The first task in doing tax research is to understand the organization of the Code and Regulations. The Code is organized in a series of headings and subheadings, which, on the surface, appear very complex. A sample of these headings is given on the next page, in descending order from a very broad heading to a very narrow, specific section:

INTERNAL REVENUE CODE

Subtitle A Income Taxes
  Chapter 1 Normal Taxes & Surtaxes
      Subchapter A Determination of Tax
      Liability Part I Tax on Individuals
        Subpart A Nonrefundable
        Personal Credits

          Section 1 to 9602
            Subsection (a)
            Paragraph(1)
                Subparagraph (A)
                Clause (i)

The dotted line would not actually appear in the Code headings, but it has been added here to make the following point. The entire series of headings which appear above the dotted line (Subtitle A: Income Taxes through Subpart A: Nonrefundable Personal Credits) can be ignored for most research purposes. This is because the headings called "Sections" (below the dotted line) are numbered independently and do not depend on the bradiersheadings above them. The first section of the Internal Revenue Code is Section 1, and the last is Section +9600. Thus the tax researcher need only locate the proper Section to read without referring to the Subtitle, Subchapter, or Subpart, which that Section belongs to.

Then the researcher must find the proper paragraph or clause in the Code, using the headings indicated below the dotted line. For example, what if the researcher wanted to locate Internal Revenue Code Section 6104(e)? They would need to use the Code and find the page, which contains the heading "Section 6104(e)" at the bottom left-hand corner. If they wanted to find IRC Sec. 6104(e)(l) (B)(ii), they would simply follow the subheadings on the page containing Section 6104(e) as one would follow the pattern of any ordinary outline. In this example, Sec. 6104(e)(l)(B)(ii) would be referred to as Section 6104, Subsection e, Paragraph 1, Subparagraph B, Clause ii.)

What if the researcher wanted to locate provisions of the Code allowing for, say, public inspection of a nonprofit organization's financial information; the code section that makes a financial service such as GuideStar possible, http://www.guidestar.org.[4] This is an example of topical research and it demands a little more effort than locating a Section citation as in the previous case. The researcher would open the Code to the outline in the front and look for the Subtitle covering tax-exempt activities (in this case, Subtitle F). Then the appropriate Section could be found in Subtitle F, based on the Sections' titles. Section 6104's title is PUBLICITY OF INFORMATION REQUIRED FROM CERTAIN EXEMPT ORGANIZATIONS AND CERTAIN TRUSTS. Subsection 6104(e) is entitled, "Public Inspection of Certain Annual Returns and Applications for Exemption." These titles serve as signposts guiding the researcher to the part of the Code that addresses their tax question. The Code follows a format somewhat more complex than the chapter and verse designations of the Holy Bible. Each Section of the Code is commonly referred to as a "cite" which is short for citation. When this dissertation refers to 501(c)(3), it means IRC section 501, Subsection c, Paragraph 3. This is a cite.

This is how the Code is organized, but what about the organization of the Internal Revenue Regulations? The Regulations follow a system of headings similar to the Code. Just place a "1" in front of the Code Section in use and you will know the proper Regulations to read. For example, the Regulations on organizations discussed in Code Section 501(c)(3) are found in Regulation Sec. l.501(c)(3). However, that is as far as the similarity between the Code and Regulations goes. The Subsection numbers in the Code, for example, are not equivalent to Regulation citations. Apart from the Section headings, the Regulations are organized differently from the Code. Most of the time a researcher will need to browse the Regulation Section which addresses the tax question to find the proper Regulation.

The Master Tax Guide

There is an abbreviated way to do tax research. A Master Tax Guide has been designed for the U.S. to assist researchers in locating tax research information quickly and easily. Both the IRC and the Master Tax Guide have an identical topical index. The Master Tax Guide can be ordered from CCH. Most professional tax researchers know the IRC so well that they can go to the proper section without an index. But most beginning tax researchers prefer the index in the Master Tax Guide over the index in the IRC because it is more user-friendly. The topical index of the Master Tax Guide gives a brief description of the law and regulations related to a researcher's question, helping him or her find the proper Code section or Regulation. The Master Tax Guide also gives information on court cases pertaining to various tax questions.

The Commerce Clearing House (CCH) version of the Master Tax Guide will also refer researchers to another type of tax publication, the CCH Standard Federal Tax Reports. These Federal Tax Reports discuss specific tax questions in detail, such as pension and employee benefits, automobile deductions or state taxes. The tax reports are produced by tax services such as CCH and are marketed to CPA firms and law firms in the U.S. to assist them in doing tax research. There are many tax services (other than CCH) offering such publications. Most research experts agree that the Bureau of National Affairs (BNA) is the most comprehensive of the tax services.

The Research Institute of America (RIA) is a newcomer to the tax research area and will not be found in the list of tax service providers in most law libraries. Most attorneys prefer BNA and it often includes sample forms for the legal profession to use. RIA is very popular with CPA firms. Either of these services, as well as CCH, can be helpful to the practicing accountant.

Tax Services
Here is a list of the major tax services and the titles of their respective tax report publications:

Bureau of National Affairs(BNA)
>   Tax Management Portfolios

Commerce Clearing House(CCH)
>   Standard Federal Tax Reporter
>   Tax Treaties
>   Federal Estate & Gift Tax Reports

Prentice-Hall (PH)
>   Federal Taxes
>   Federal Taxes—Estate & Gift Taxes
>   Tax—Exempt Organizations

Research Institute of America(RIA)
>   Federal Tax Coordinator 2d

The practicing accountant will usually find the Code and Regulations to be of sufficient detail to meet his or her needs. However, the Regulations are written with a particular bias (the collection of tax), which the tax services will help the researcher to see through or around. This insight into ways of using the regulations to the researcher's advantage is referred to as "tax planning." Tax planning is what accountants and attorneys charge significant fees to perform.

Legal Precedent – Court decisions are just as binding as the code
If what has been explained so far were the whole story, tax research would be simple. The researcher would only need the books and services mentioned above. Unfortunately, the real world is an imperfect place, and U.S. Congressmen are imperfect persons. (This is no surprise to voters). When the U.S. Congress makes the tax laws, it does not always anticipate all the ways in which those laws will be applied, interpreted and scrutinized for loopholes. Who gets to settle the disputes over the interpretation of the Code and Regulations? The

court system, of course, is the mechanism for resolving disputes between taxpayers and the Internal Revenue Service (IRS). Interestingly, the IRS is almost always the defendant in tax cases. The IRS does not need the court system to impound a checking account or place a lien against a taxpayer's property. The taxpayer, however, does need the court system to get relief from the strong arm of the IRS.

If an individual or organization pays a tax and then files for a refund, which the IRS refuses to pay, the taxpayer may have to request a trial. In this situation, the case would go to a District Court. If, on the other hand, the taxpayer <u>does</u> <u>not</u> pay the tax and desires to defend his or her action, the taxpayer must take the case to litigation. This may lead to a trial in Tax Court. Tax Court cases are legal proceedings before a single judge who will also review the case with other justices. Tax Court cases are not jury trials. Some of the best tax experts in the nation sit as justices on the Tax Court.

Most tax cases are disputes over interpretation of the law. The Tax Court has the authority to rule on several cases at once by deciding a particular case, which is similar to others. Unlike Tax Court rulings, rulings by a District Court are only binding within that court's judicial district and they have no impact on decisions in other districts. At the time a tax dispute goes to Tax Court, another individual or organization at an earlier point in time may have faced the same tax question. If the same issue has been litigated already, then the results of the earlier case might be ruled as binding on the case that is currently before the court. The court must follow legal precedent. Tax research through the study of court cases requires the use of parallelism.

Court decisions play a major role in determining how tax laws are to be carried out. Congress does not go back and revise the Code for each omission that it makes in tax law (and only on very rare occasions does it codify a court case). Instead, Congress is quite content to let the court system work out the finer details of how the law is applied. After all, Congress does not want to handle the often-heated political issues that come up as the law goes into effect. It is for the courts to straighten out the problems created by Congress. Thus court justices, in deciding a case, will go back to Congressional records to search for the intent of Congress in making the law. This is a difficult process and explains in part the current backlog of cases faced by the court system.

A typical example of the search for congressional intent in a tax case is that of a taxpayer challenging an IRS regulation. The issue before the court is whether or not the regulation at hand went beyond the scope of Congress' intention at the time it was put into effect by the Treasury Department. Many times tax researchers must also resolve a tax question by searching for the intent of Congress. This can be done by studying the Congressional Records, which recount the steps taken by Congress in enacting a law. These steps can provide clues as to Congress' intent in making a law.

U.S. taxpayers should view the Tax Court as the protector of their rights as U.S. citizens. Tax Courts are designed to give each tax case a fair and thorough review in order to render a just verdict.

Research of Case Law

Most of the tax services mentioned earlier refer readers to selected court cases on critical tax questions, and give an overview of the results of each case. But what if the tax service doesn't provide any court cases on the topic being researched? How does the researcher find appropriate case material? Most of the time, tax researchers who are interested in any topic in general can find the court cases they need in what is called a "citator." This' is a separate published document which indexes court cases according to the tax questions they address. The best and most popular of the court case citators is called "Shepard's Federal Tax Citations." The major tax services also publish their own citators. Unfortunately, using a citator can be extremely tedious. For years, most tax researchers thought there had to be a better way.

Thankfully, there is a better way! That better way is to use an electronic data base service. All of the transcripts of every tax case in the U.S. have been entered into full—text computer software that can do a word search and locate specific court cases in a matter of seconds. These electronic libraries can provide a complete listing of all the court cases and journal articles on virtually any tax question. The volume of information these database services provide can be overwhelming. Individuals or organizations can purchase time on one of these legal databases using their own computers and a modem. The cost for these services can be prohibitive for most individual users, unless they have clients to bill for their services. Many CPA firms and law firms purchase time from these services regularly.

Electronic database services

All of the major tax services offer web-based tax research. Lexis-Nexis is still considered the premier service, but it is also the most expensive. Many college, university, and public libraries subscribe to Lexis-Nexis and allow outside web access to their site. This means it is possible to find free web access, through a library site, to the most powerful tax database available over the web. Simply search the web for Lexis-Nexis Academic Universe and library sites will be available to you. Smaller libraries only permit access to Lexis-Nexis if you are on campus or protect the web access with passwords.

The most popular site to accountants is RIA (Research Institute of America) and their research database called "checkpoint." One nice feature about RIA is the upfront pricing, special offers, and a 30 day free trial http://www.riag.com/. They also aggressively market to academic institutions, offering free service to students for one semester as a means of their becoming familiar with RIA products.

Popular among legal professionals is West Publishing, which offers "WestDoc" as a tax research database http://www.westdoc.com/. The great thing about WestDoc is the billing. They charge $10.00 per document after you complete a registration form and agree to the "WestDoc Subscriber Agreement." Also very popular among the legal profession is a site maintained by Tax Analysts. Their database is called "TaxBase" and can be found at http://www.tax.org/. They are very upfront about the pricing. Federal tax research is $349.95 and you can add other services for a minimal fee. Tax Analysts also has a free trial offer.

As previously mentioned, the publishing backbone of the tax research world is CCH Incorporated. The online store for CCH is http://onlinestore.cch.com. Their list of tax research publications is extensive. Their online research product is called CCH Internet℠ Tax Research NetWork™ and can be found at: http://tax.cchgroup.com/taxresearchnetwork/main.asp. Unfortunately their pricing for tax research is not available over the web. You have to talk to a sales representative.

Most of the databases present the search options in terms of different books or a library of research volumes. Each book represents a set of materials that can be searched electronically. The Code and Regulations, for example, represents one of the books. The Master Tax Guide or a student's textbook represents another book to search. The key to any electronic search is the key words used in the search. Too many words in the search will create the possibility of missing the topic and too few words mean an excessive number of search results to read. Electronic tax research is an art form that takes practice. There is more advice about electronic searches in the section entitled Substantial Authority.

Hard Copy Research

Tax court cases are also stored in published reference volumes. You will find that the citations used to locate specific cases will direct you to these reference volumes for information. Each volume contains the full text of a range of court cases. Each volume is published by a court reporting service and carries the name of that service. Similarly, every court citation includes the name of a court reporting service in abbreviated form. The name of the court reporting service in a court citation will signal the tax court case volume for which to look. The electronic database searches will also reference the same citations.

Below are some examples of court citations and the court reporting services to which they refer:

Cite listing	Court Reporting Service
S. Ct.	Supreme Court Reporter
AFTR	American Federal Tax Reports
USTC	U.S. Tax Cases
L. Ed.	United States Supreme Court Reports, Lawyers's Edition
U.S.	United States Reports
F.	Federal Reported
F.Supp.	Federal Supplement
Ct.Cl.	U.S. Court of Claims
TCM	Tax Court Memorandum
B.T.A.	Board of Tax Appeals Reports

Each court reporting service uses the same cover on all of its court case volumes. For this reason, finding the proper series of volumes in a law library can be a challenge. But once the researcher locates the proper set of volumes with the librarian's help, one should have little trouble finding the particular volume and page number with the court case needed. If the researcher only wants to check the general issue involved in a court case, then it is helpful to look at the short syllabus, which (in almost all cases) precedes that case.

Administrative Materials

The Internal Revenue Code consists of tax laws issued by Congress. As such, the Code is a legislative document. However, the Internal Revenue Regulations published by the U.S. Department of the Treasury are an administrative document. In addition to the Regulations, the Treasury Department often issues "revenue rulings" (abbreviated Rev. Rul.) and "revenue procedures" (Rev. Proc.). These statements allow the Internal Revenue Service to communicate its position on specific tax questions to the public without having to issue new regulations. Often, the Rev.Rul. and Rev.Proc. may come as a result of questions by several taxpayers or as a result of court cases. They are published weekly in the Internal Revenue Bulletin. A summary of these weekly bulletins comes out every (quarter/year) in a document called the "Cumulative Bulletin." The tax services and court reporting services will often refer to the Cumulative Bulletin, allowing the researcher to find Rev.Rul. and Rev.Proc. related to their tax question.

One might be particularly interested in reading a Rev.Rul. and Rev.Proc. during a major tax court case. For example, if the IRS litigates a case and happens to loose the case, the IRS can announce nonacquiescence on the issue in the Rev.Ruling. This nonacquiescence means that if the IRS lost the case in one district, it will still litigate the issue in a different district. The IRS can loose in several court districts (or circuits) and still win the overall court battle by appealing its best case to a higher court. Sometimes the IRS or a taxpayer appeals all the way to the Supreme Court.

Substantial Authority

Now to review the sequence for doing tax research under the U.S. system. Start with the index in the Code, the Master Tax Guide, or any other tax service guide. If an electronic database is available, selecting the key words for the search is the critical issue. It is highly efficient in an electronic search to start with more key words than might be necessary, thereby limiting the search to a very specific set of documents. If the search does not yield a match of key words within the same paragraph, then the key words are reduced by the least important word and the search is initiated for the second time. Generally, it is recommended to begin a search with the Master Tax Guide or with a tax textbook, so that the first explanation is the most complete. Next, search and read the relevant Code Section and Regulations. If more detail is needed, search for court cases and /or Rev.Rul. / Rev.Proc. related to the tax issue in question.

Manual searching also involves the selection of key words from the index. Sometimes a novice researcher will use a manual index to perform a general survey of the topic being considered thereby establishing the key concepts (words) at issue and then begin the electronic database search.

Researchers in such a complex system may have trouble resisting the temptation to skip over the Code and Regulations in favor of the more readable tax service publications. This strategy is ill advised because not all tax research carries the same weight with the IRS when penalties are being assessed or when tax disputes are being resolved in court. To the court system a regulation carries the full authority of a legal brief. And to the IRS the Regulations carry the weight of law. Therefore, if the position taken by the taxpayer is based on the Regulations, the Code, or a reported court case, the taxpayer will be in a better position to avoid a penalty from the IRS. If the authority for the action comes from one of the tax services such as RIA, it will not be regarded as "substantial authority" and may result in a penalty. Those who teach tax research will generally assign a grade based on the quality or "substantial authority" documented by the student

The ONLY Sources, which give substantial authority, are:

Legislative
Administrative
Judicial

Secondary Sources are the tax services or textbook descriptions. The IRS is not impressed with ideas, opinion, or tax planning tips found in these services. The taxpayer will be at his or her own risk if he or she fails to provide Code, regulation, or judicial decisions to defend a tax position.

Bibliography

Blacks Law Dictionary, by Henry Campbell Black M.A. West Publishing Co. St. Paul Minn. (This dictionary is to the legal profession what the Webster dictionary is to most office people — An absolute necessity!)

Federal' Tax Research. Guide to Materials and
    Techniques, 3rd. Ed. Gail Levin Richmond, Foundation Press, N.Y.

Legal Research in a Nutshell, Morris Cohen, West
    Publishing Co., St Paul, MINN.

The Legal Research Manual. A game plan for legal
    research and analysis, Wren, Published by A-R Editions Inc., Madison, Wisconsin.

Prentice—Hall Federal Taxes, Englewood Cliffs, NJ
    07632

Research Institute of America. Inc. 90 Fifth Avenue,
    N.Y. N.Y. 10011

Using American Law Books, Alfred J. Lewis,
    Kendall/Hunt Pub. Co. Dubuque, Iowa.

West's Law Finder. A research manual for lawyers,
    West Publishing Co. P.O.Box 64526, St. Paul, MINN. 55164—9979

[1] Matt 22:21 <u>The New Jerusalem Bible</u>, Doubleday, N.Y. 1966.

[2] Ibid, Romans 13.

[3] Ibid, Luke 16:9-13

[4] Guide Star provides financial information on nonprofit organizations. The site also has a copy of the Form 990 available using *Acrobat Reader*, for most nonprofits.

PUBLIC CHARITY or PRIVATE FOUNDATION

What does it mean to be a 501(c)(3) organization

By

Dr. Jack E. Bower

Eastern University

God has blessed the U.S.A. beyond imagination. Particularly well blessed is the nonprofit sector which now represents about 30% of the U.S. economy. The most common type of nonprofit organizations are public charities, which includes the church and countless Christian ministries. The most critical functions in American society are performed by public charities ranging from medicine to education. The most important functions of the church are also being performed by Christian ministries.

"I tell you the truth, whatever you did for one of the least of these brothers of mine, you did for me....... For I was hungry and you gave me nothing to drink. I was a stranger and you did not invite me in, I needed cloths and you did not clothe me, I was sick and in prison and you did not look after me." Many U.S. churches focus primarily on spiritual needs. Those concerned about this description of the judgement day will often organize themselves into public charities to meet **both** spiritual and physical needs. The poor and needy all around the world are being directly impacted by U.S. based development organizations as they seek to meet the needs of others.

Every Christian accountant concerned about ministry outside the church need to understand the fundamental tax concepts governing the qualifications necessary to obtain and maintain public charity status. The continuation of the Lords work through various ministries depends on continued public charity status. Unfortunately this topic is highly technical in nature. The formulas presented in this chapter are used by the U.S. Internal Revenue Service (IRS) to determine public charity status and are sometimes not fully understood even by those who practice accounting or law.

The Favorable Tax Environment

Estate taxation has fueled the U.S. nonprofit sector. From the Revenue Act of 1916 until the repeal starting in 2002, wealthy families have had two choices. Give a significant portion of the estate, about 55%, to the federal government in taxes or form a private foundation to administer the wealth.[1] Most would choose to form a private foundation and then have their children benefit as trustees. Private foundations must give 5% of their assets to public charities or spend 5% themselves on charitable activities. Most choose to fund public charities by awarding grants. Hence a significant amount of funding is available to public charities who properly apply for it. However, the tax incentive to form a private foundation has now changed. In June of 2001 President Bush signed into law a 1.35 trillion dollar tax cut. Part of the tax reduction package was the phase-out of the estate tax over time with a total repeal by the year 2010. A coalition of nonprofit organizations is fighting the phase-out and repeal. Their website is http://www.ombwatch.org.

Tax laws also favor the giving of property to public charities. The amount of the donation (and deduction) is equal to the fair market value of the property regardless of the price paid for the property. Gifts of appreciated property avoid capital gains tax and provide a shield from paying income tax in the form of a charitable contribution deduction.

Once Exempt Always Exempt?

Many accountants and managers of nonprofit public charities assume that their "public charity" status is irrevocable, not realizing that every two years, the IRS reviews the records (on Form 990) submitted by each 501(c)(3) organization to determine whether or not it still qualifies as a public charity. If the organization no longer qualifies, the organization may be forced into the less desirable status of a "private foundation." The IRS can revoke exemption without a hearing.[2]

The Difference Between Public Charities and Private Foundations

What is the difference between a public charity and a private foundation, and why is there a problem if an organization loses its status as a public charity and becomes a private foundation? All 501(c)(3) organizations are classified as either public charities or private foundations. The difference between these two types of 501(c)(3) organizations is almost as great as the difference between the government of the U.S. and China. Private foundations must give away a certain percentage of their assets each year. Penalties for noncompliance with this rule are severe and can be imposed on both the manager(s) and the organization itself. No such restriction exists for public charities.

Congress created these harsh restrictions for private foundations because it perceived that wealthy individuals were using private foundations as a front for amassing huge private fortunes tax-free. Critics have called the rules for private foundations "overkill." But whether the rules go too far or not, they can create such an administrative headache that any 501(c)(3) organization that does not intend to operate as a private foundation should therefore guard its public charity status at all costs.

The situation is further complicated by the fact that the IRS also has imposed strict requirements on 501(c)(3) organizations registered as public charities. If a public charity fails to comply with IRS requirements, it can be penalized by being turned into a private foundation automatically. This is considered a penalty precisely because of the heavy load of restrictions imposed on private foundations.

How easy is it for an organization to lose its public charity status? In some cases, very easy! The U.S. congress created a set of rules to make sure public charities have a broad base of public support. Basically, all a public charity has to do to get in trouble with the IRS is receive one or two very large gifts from an outside source. The IRS tries to make this point clear on its form 990 but, many accountants who complete these forms with detailed financial information about their organizations do not realize how the IRS intends to use it to determine their eligibility to remain a public charity.

What Constitutes a Public Charity?

Public charities and private foundations are defined in the Internal Revenue Code section 501(c)(3). There are many types of nonprofit organizations but only 501(c)(3) organizations can accept tax deductible charitable contributions. There are basically five tests necessary to become an exempt organization as defined in IRS regulation 1.509 & 1.501(c)(3)-1:

Organizational and operational tests. Commonly referred to as the purpose test. Does the organization have an exempt purpose? First there is the paper test. Do the Articles of Incorporation and Bylaws clearly state the charitable purpose? Next is the smell test. Does the organization really and truly operate for a charitable purpose?

No private inurement. The word inurement means getting use to something over time. The IRS uses this word to refer to individuals becoming accustomed to receiving personal benefits from a nonprofit organization. It is also a Biblical concept. Over time, we can be seduced by sin into thinking that nothing is wrong. The point is that there can be no distribution of earning in any form to individuals or private shareholders.

No propaganda to influence legislation. The political activities of nonprofit organizations are extremely limited. There is a fine line between distribution of information on a topic and trying to influence legislation.

The assets must be dedicated for an exempt purpose. One of the critical tests will be the distribution of the assets on dissolution. It must be clearly stated in the articles of incorporation that the assets upon dissolution will go to another organization "to be uses in such a manner as (in the judgment of the court) will best accomplish the general purpose for which (the dissolved organization was organized.)" [3]

Public support test to determine public charity or private foundation status. The eligibility criteria for organizations seeking public charity status are complex but extremely critical if applicants are to avoid private foundation status. Public charities must pass one of a set of "tests" designed by the IRS to make sure they have a broad support base. If they do not satisfy one of the tests, then they are automatically a private foundation. In other words, they must seek qualification as a public charity and actively maintain that qualification. The tests are found in section 509(a) of the Internal Revenue Code. The reminder of this chapter will outline the four basic tests used by the IRS.

The Tests of IRC Section 509(a)

"For purposes of this title, the term private foundation means a domestic or foreign organization described in section 501(c)(3) other than [the following tests].."(Section 509).

An organization seeking public charity status must meet any one of the following tests. An organization is not required to pass more than one test to qualify.

Test #1 is entitled "Reason for Non-Private Foundation Status" and is found in section 509(a)(l). This test has two parts. **Part One** of the test names specific types of organizations that can qualify automatically as public charities simply by virtue of the type of organization they are. This part of the Code states that:

"Any organizations described in section 170(b)(l)(A) of the IRC other than in clauses (vii) and (viii)" are public charities. In other words, in order to be eligible to receive charitable contributions, an organization must be described in 170(b)(l)(A). (Section 170 is part of a long section of permissible tax deductions.)

Sec.170(b)(l)(A) of the Code includes a list of organizations as follows:

(vi) a church or a convention or association of churches

(ii) an educational organization which normally maintains a regular faculty and curriculum and normally has a regularly enrolled body of pupils

(iii) an organization the principal purpose or functions of which are the providing of medical or hospital care or medical education or medical research

(iv) organizations which operate exclusively to serve state colleges. (This is a paraphrase of the law.) This section was created for the land grant state colleges.

(v) a governmental unit

(vi) an organization referred to in subsection 170(c)(2) which normally receives a substantial part of its support ... from a governmental unit ... or from direct or indirect contributions from the general public.

Test #1, part one, provides public charity status to four types of nonprofits. Churches, educational institutions, governmental agencies, and medical organizations which are exempt from tax by definition. Church organizations in these categories generally do not have to be concerned about losing their public charity status.

What about an organization which is not a part of the prior list of organizations that automatically qualifies? Those organizations, not listed above in (i) through (vi), must meet the conditions of subpart (vi) of Section 170. This is the **second part** of Test #1. The Internal Revenue Regulations use a specific formula to determine whether or not an organization is receiving a *"substantial part of its support"* from a broad public base. The formula is applied to nonprofits that are neither churches, schools, government agencies, nor medical organizations.

The formula, described in Regulation 1.170A-9(e)(7), aims to determine that a minimum of one third of an organization's total financial support is from the general public. This test is commonly referred to as the "one-third" (or thirty-three and one— third percent) support test. In any organization, the ratio of public to total support must be thirty-three and one-third percent or more in order for the organization to qualify as a public charity. Congress wants to make sure that public charities are not being used by only a few large donors as a refuge from taxes. This public-support formula is Congress' plumb line.

Schedule A, Part IV, box 11
The IRS builds this one-third support ratio (or fraction) using financial information provided to the IRS on Form 990, Schedule A, Part IV box 11 and Part IV-A, lines 26, a to f. The tax regulations specify what types of support an organization should include in this fraction when it is trying to determine whether it qualifies as a public

charity. To qualify as a public charity, an organization should aim to include as much revenue in the numerator of the fraction as possible in order to achieve the required one-third percentage. The calculation from the data it provides on Form 990 is clearly defined as the public support percentage and the organization should know immediately if it has fallen below the one-third-support threshold. Note that the calculation is based on four, years of data because the IRS uses a four-year average of revenue to determine the fraction.

Here is a summary of the box 11 test, found on Part IV-A, lines 15 to 26, Schedule A Form 990:

IRC 509(a)(1)
IRC 170 (b)(1)(A)(vi)
IRS Regulations 1.70A-9(e)(7)
"More than 33 1/3 Support Test" on a 4-year moving total

SOURCE OF SUPPORT	NUMERATOR	DENOMINATOR
Gifts, Grants, Contributions:		
From Qualified Sources …………..	**include**	**include**
All government grants (not contracts)	**include**	**include**
From all other 170(b)(1)(A) organizations	**include**	**include**
From Disqualified Sources (amount over 2% of Total Support over four years)	**exclude**	**include**
Membership Fees:		
To belong to the organization ……….	**include**	**include**
To purchase a service or merchandise	**exclude**	**include**

ORGANIZATIONS THAT DEPEND PRIMARILY ON GROSS RECEIPTS OR GOVERNMENT CONTRACTS FOR THEIR FINANCIAL SUPPORT MUST USE THE 509 (a)(2) TEST.

Gross Receipts from related activities:

Sales of merchandise	**exclude**	**exclude**
Performance of a service	**exclude**	**exclude**
Furnishing of facilities	**exclude**	**exclude**
Admission fees	**exclude**	**exclude**

Gross Receipts from unrelated business activities.

exclude	**include**

Government Contracts for public facilities such as
    Libraries, Nursing Homes, Child Care

include	**include**

(Significant research grants will force the
use of the 509(a)(2) test.)

Gross Investment Income .... **exclude**   **include**

Contribution of services (Donated services) **exclude**   **exclude**

Support from a feeder organization:

509(a)(3) organization	**exclude**	**exclude**
509(a)(3) organization	**include**	**include**

IF THE NUMERATOR, DIVIDED BY THE DOMINATOR is more than 33 1/3, the organization passes the public support test.

    The regulations also provide for another test under 509(a)(1), 170(b)(1)(A)(vi). This test is commonly referred to as the facts and circumstances test under test #1. It is the test of last resort. This test is for organizations that fail all other tests for being a public charity under test #1 or test #2.

    To be considered under the facts and circumstances test, an organization must have at least ten percent public support. Of course public support would be less than thirty-three and one-third. The result is that the IRS must make a judgment call. All the organization can do is present the facts in a manner favorable to the organization and pray for good results. The IRS is not adversarial in dealing with nonprofits regarding the support test. The revenue agent might even suggest some changes that will improve the case for public charity status. Here is a brief outline of test:

FACTS AND CIRCUMSTANCES TEXT

Ten percent is the minimal requirement to be considered under the facts and circumstances rule.

If the 10% test is met, the next issue is actual and planned solicitation.

Is the organization organized and operated to attract public and government support on a continuing basis?

Is the scope of fund raising activities reasonable in light of activities?

Is it a lack of start-up funding keeping the organization from expanding their solicitation program?

Endowment – If from a few individuals – unfavorable

If from the government or general public – favorable

Does the governing body represent the broad interest of the general public? Community leaders and public officials are viewed as representing the public interest.

Does the organization provide facilities or services directly for the benefit of the general public on a continual basis?

Does the general public participate in the organization's activities?

This is a brief overview of the test. Consult the regulations for a complete summary.

Test #2 is found in Code Section 509(a)(2). This test is another support test. Organizations can use Test #2 if they do not qualify as public charities under Test #1. Organizations which do not qualify by virtue of the type of organization they are, must qualify by how they are supported. An organization does not qualify as a public charity on the basis of what it does. This is a common misconception!

Schedule A, Part IV, box 12

Like test #1, test #2 has two parts. The first part of Test #2 is commonly referred to as the "more than one-third support test." This is the same formula as that used under Test #1 with two differences. First, the formula used in Test #1 is called the "thirty three and one third" support test (meaning 33 1/3 percent), whereas the formula in Test #2, part 1 is called the "one third" support test. There is no difference here in terms of mathematics but only in terms of labeling. The real difference is that organizations that depend PRIMARILY on income from fees for services they perform must use the 509(a)(2) formula. Thus, the Test #1 formula applies to organizations with only donated (i.e., not earned) income.

The second part of the second test sets a maximum limit rather than a minimum limit. In this part of test #2, the part of an organization's income that comes from unrelated business activities and investments cannot exceed one third of that organization's total support. If it does, the organization fails this test. Organizations can deduct business-related expenses from their business income in this calculation. Here is a summary of the second test as found on Schedule A, Part IV box 12 and Part IV-A lines 27, a to h:

IRC 509 (a)(2) TEST
More than one-third of support
On a four-year moving average
Regulation 1.509(a)-3

SOURCE OF SUPPORT   **NUMBERATOR   DENOMINATOR**

Gifts, Grants, Contributions:

	NUMBERATOR	DENOMINATOR
From Qualified Sources......	**include**	include
All government grants (not contracts)	**include**	include
From all 170(b)(1)(A) organizations	**include**	include
From Disqualified Sources (gives over	**exclude**	include

$5000. in total from all years OR an amount
over 1% of Total Support over four years)
(Exclude **larger** of amount **over** $5000 or 1% from any one
source)

Membership Fees:
　　To support the organization …**include**　　　　**include**
　　To purchase a service or merchandise
　　　　　　…... **include**　　　　**include**
(Exclude **larger** of amounts **over** $5000 or 1% from any one
source)

Gross Receipts from **related** activities:
　　Sales of merchandise …….. **include**　　　　**include**
　　Performance of a service… **include**　　　　**include**
　　Furnishing of facilities …… **include**　　　　**include**
　　Admission fees …………... **include**　　　　**include**
(Exclude **larger** of amounts **over** $5000 or 1% from any one
source)

Gross Receipts from unrelated business activities.
　　　　　　　　　　exclude　　　　**include**
　　Exceptions:
　　Sales for the convenience of members
　　Sales using all volunteer labor
　　Selling of donated merchandise

Gross Investment Income(Interest, Royalties, Rents)
　　　　　　　　　　exclude　　　　**include**
GROSS INVESTMENT INCOME CANNOT EXCEED 1/3 OF
TOTAL SUPPORT

Capital gains on Sale of Property ….**exclude**　　　　**exclude**

Contribution of services (Donated services) …….
　　　　　　　　　　exclude　　　　**exclude**

IF THE NUMERATOR, DIVIDED BY THE DOMINATOR is more than one-third, the organization passes the public support test.

Test #3 is found in section 509(a)(3) of the Code. Organizations that qualify under this test have a parent organization that is already a public charity. The supporting organization must exclusively serve the parent in order to qualify under this test.

Test #4 is a test for organizations which test for public safety and is found in 509(a)(4).

Interrelationship of the Tests

The material at the end of this chapter presents a summary outline of the tests for public charity status. The concepts seem very simple but the application of these concepts can be very complex. Those who work in this area on a daily basis refer to public charity status as a "form of art" because there are many various shades of meaning associated with these Code sections and Regulations.

Which test has priority in the IRS' evaluation? Some organizations will qualify under more than one test. However, the IRS' determination letter will always use the 509(a)(1) test if the organization qualifies under more than one test. The organization selects the test it wants the IRS to use by checking the proper box on Form 990, Schedule A. Most will choose box 11 or 12 as outlined above. The significance of these boxes is not clear on the 990 Schedule A, but the instructions for Form 990 Schedule A are helpful. Following are some terms in the IRS Code and Regulations that are critical to an understanding of the public charity tests.

Qualified Source[4]

Not everyone who gives to a public charity is actually helping the organization. Large grant makers are very aware of the damage they can do to a public charity. If a grant from one source is too large, it can cause an organization to fail the 509(a) tests and lose its public charity status. Interestingly, in such a case, the IRS can impose severe penalties on the donor as well as the public charity. Thus, many foundation grants require matching funds from the public at large. The grant givers are not only interested in protecting the public charities that receive their grants; they are protecting themselves!

How does a public charity determine whether an incoming gift or grant is too large? The first issue to be addressed is "Substantial Contributor" as defined under 507(d)(2). If the donor is a substantial contributor, the gift will be considered as being from a disqualified source and therefore not counted in the public support portion of the fraction under the code for test #2.

A second group of disqualified donors are the "Disqualified Persons" as defined in 4946 (a). All major donors and board members must be reviewed against these two legislative standards for exclusion from public support under test #2. If the donor is excluded from public support, the entire amount of their gift is excluded. Therefore, organizations must be very careful which test they are using and under which standards they evaluate their donors.

Test #1, part 2 (the thirty-three and one third support test as defined in the regulations, not the code), states that no gift from any one source may exceed 2 percent of the organization's total support. Any amount above the 2 percent threshold is excluded from the organization's public support base. In other words, part of the gift of a qualified source does not count towards public support if they exceed the 2% threshold. In test #2, part 1, the threshold for qualified sources is only one percent. Please note the 1% test is for qualified sources not disqualified sources.

Form 990, Schedule A asks for the calculation of the 2% and 1% thresholds that are used to determine who is qualified or not qualified as a public source on the Support Schedule, Part IV-A, lines 25 and 26. Another critical point regarding the 2% test is that it is based **on cumulative donations** over time. Form 990 stipulates that the organization add the contribution of each source over a four-year moving average. This adding of all the years' gifts for each contributor is what many organizations fail to do until audited.

In the test #2, the Schedule A threshold for individual sources is 1 percent of an organization's total revenue OR $5,000., whichever is larger. For example, if total revenue was $100,000, then the $5,000 would be the benchmark not 1% of $100,000 which is $1,000. If the gift was 6,000, then 5,000 of this gift would be included in the tally of public support. If the gift was 4,000, then the full $4,000 would be included in the public support base. If total revenue was $1,000,000 then $10,000 would be the benchmark for inclusion in the numerator of the support fraction (the public support measure).

Once a donor becomes disqualified, he or she remains disqualified until they pass the "good boy" test. The "good boy" test is found in IRC Section 507(d)(2)(C). If the disqualified contributor does not give anything to the public charity for the next ten years nor is involved in management of the organization, then that person can again become a qualified donor. The point Congress is making is very obvious; Congress does not want an individual person or organization to have control of public charities. The organization must be responsive to the general public rather than the private interests of one individual or family.

It is very important to note that unlike test #2, which excludes the entire gift of a disqualified donor, the 2% test of test #1 only excludes the amount over the 2%. This means that at least some of the gift is included in the numerator when calculating the 33 & 1/3 support test in test #1.

Unusual Grants

Unusual grants can be excluded from both public and total support if they meet certain criteria.[5]

(i)   Are attracted by reason of the publicly supported nature of the organization;

(ii)   Are unusual or unexpected with respect to the amount thereof; and

(iii)   Would by the reason of their size, adversely affect the status of the organization as normally meeting the one-third support test for any of the applicable periods described in paragraph

The calculation should be done using **cash accounting.** However, generally accepted accounting principles require the accrual method of accounting. Some adjusting may be necessary if the preparer of Form 990 is using audited financial statements as the source of financial information, as these statements use accrual accounting. The first adjustment for unusual grants would be to remove the entry "grant receivable" from revenue because it is recorded but not actually received. The second adjustment would be to add back to revenue the amount received during the year, but classified as "deferred revenue.

Some disqualified donors will try giving their gifts to another public charity to keep the charitable contribution deduction on their personal income tax return. They then have the funds earmarked for the public charity from which they have been disqualified. There is a regulation that prohibits this kind of transaction, but discovery by the IRS is almost impossible.

Summary of the four tests:

Test #1 509(a)(1) The organization is described in 170(b)(1)(A)

i	a church or association of churches
ii	an educational organization
iii	medical or hospital
iv	in support of a state college
v	a governmental unit
vi	33&1/3% public support or facts & circumstances test

Test #2 509(a)(2) Public Support Tests:

more than one-third test

Numerator = permitted sources
Denominator = total support that is not
          disqualified

less than one-third test:

Net U.B.I. + Investment Income
Total support that is not disqualified

Test #3 509(a)(3) Public charity status because of relationship to another public charity such as a church, IRS Income Tax Regulation 1.6033-2(g)(1)(vii).

Test #4 509(a)(4) Testing for public safety

[1] Paragraph 42, 1999 U.S. Master Tax Guide.

[2] Metzger Est.,100 TC No.14.

[3] IRS Regulation 1.501(c)(3)-4.

[4] I.R.C. 4946(a)(2)

[5] Reg. 1.509(a)-3(c)(3) – Check line 28 on Schedule A, Part IV

Accounting for Solid Waste Management

By
Jack E Bower, CPA
Associate Professor of Accounting
Eastern University
&
Jonathan E. Bower
Waste Management Specialist
Pennsylvania Department of Environmental Protection[1]

I. Background

A significant group of scholars have addressed the need for more National Income Accounting measures that will track the dangers of economic over expansion.[2] This chapter focuses on the role of the Certified Public Accountant as auditor and/or consultant in the environmental debate regarding solid waste management.

The environment is a capital asset and a factor of production to all industries. For certain industries there is an ascertainable environmental degradation as a consequence of their method of production. Most noticeable is the planet's limited capacity to absorb waste. Proper waste management is a recognized responsibility mandated by society and enforced the by Environmental Protection Agency (EPA) and state agencies such as the Department of Environmental Protection (DEP)[3]. When discovered, the failure of a company to properly manage waste or the release of contaminants can result in significant fines and penalties (enforcement actions) to both the company and the accountant for violations of state and federal regulations.[4]

The proper management of waste is highly regulated and is therefore a costly and increasingly more complex process[5]. The financial impact of a non-compliant waste activity can potentially be a material item for any company and, thus, a potential unrecorded liability. It is only a matter of time until more and more responsibility for reporting the environmental liabilities comes under the scope of an audit. Even now, the A.I.C.P.A. "General Procedures" checklist instructs auditors to "obtain an understanding of the effect of laws, regulations, and ordinances having a direct and material effect on the financial statements, and prepare a list of such laws and regulations and attach it to the audit program."[6] Audit programs such as *Practitioners Clearing House* instructs auditors to determine *"Has the entity violated environmental laws? Does the entity use or generate "regulated substances" in its business?"*[7]

Accountants are familiar with depreciation, amortization and depletion. The consumption of environmental assets is called "environmental deterioration" and "resource consumption." Larger companies might employ an environmental health and safety director, a biophysical analyst, who estimates the damage or deterioration. Smaller companies can hire one of the many environmental consultants knowledgeable in biophysical analysis. These individuals can assign a dollar value to resource consumption and can recommend proper disposal methods. Some companies also establish an environmental policy. For example, Sunoco Inc. utilizes the CERES principles, which "establish an environmental ethic with criteria by which investors and others can assess the environmental performance of the company."[8] Proper management of waste is critical to reducing costs. It is always more cost effective in the long run to properly handle and lawfully dispose of waste then to pay the fines and undergo remediation penalties. If an audit forces the company to address environmental issues ahead of time the savings can be significant.

The International Organization for Standardization (ISO) encourages auditors to undergo ISO 14000 training and certification so they will be able to examine environmental management systems (EMS). ISO 14000 is a proactive approach to managing environmental problems and risks and also seeks to integrate EMS into a company's overall internal control structure. As consultants, auditors can play a critical role in voluntary compliance (compliance assistance) by assisting a company in obtaining ISO 14000 Environmental Standards Certification. The EMS audit tests "compliance with both internal and external laws, regulations and policies." The goal is to improve an organization's environmental performance by reducing resource consumption and pollution of all kinds and by protecting the environment.

II. Audit Procedures:

The key issues for auditors are (1) recognition of the

environmental risk factors and (2) determining compliance with the proper requirements.[9] Properly handling and recording an organization's waste streams is a preventive action, in contrast to the materially significant, unrecorded liabilities just waiting to explode into a major environmental incident.

For the accountant, the first step in planning is an increased awareness of the creation of waste products. The insightful accountant will see everything as a process. Every item that is manufactured, repaired and every service that interacts with the physical world is a process that creates some type of waste. Even those industries in the business of knowledge management or knowledge creation produce a paper waste. Businesses that generate problematic types of waste can be small operations such as a veterinarian or an auto dealership. Both produce waste products that require special types of disposal.

The first audit procedure in finding an unrecorded waste liability is a review of the bills or "disposal receipts" and "waste manifests." The cost of proper waste disposal is usually expensive. Does the client show an expense for waste disposal other than the local trash company? Household waste called "Municipal Waste" and construction and demolition "C&D" waste require less tracking. Other types of waste, such as industry waste, processing waste and hazardous waste require a paper trail to ensure the removal of liability as a result of proper disposal. The liability is removed when the company can document proper disposal. The paper trail can consist of disposal receipts, biennial reports, waste determinations, land disposal restriction forms and return manifests signed by a disposal facility.

A paid invoice for waste disposal, however, is not always sufficient evidence to avoid liability. A returned receipt (signed manifest) from a proper disposal site is required to insure lawful disposal for certain types of waste. This is because the original generator of the waste (generating facility) is still responsible for disposal after the waste removal or shipping company has been paid. If the waste-removal or shipping company improperly disposed of the waste, the EPA can name the generating facility as a "Partially Responsible Party" or (PRP). This is the term used by the EPA when assigning a liability for remedial action. Companies have been successfully fined years after they paid for proper disposal because they thought they sent their waste to a properly "permitted" disposal site. The shipping company as low bidder may have generated extra revenue for itself by using an improper disposal site. The key audit issue is the existence of this signed and dated "Generator Return Copy" from the original shipping manifest, which confirms proper disposal. Pennsylvania uses a hazardous waste six part form called the "Transfer Storage Disposal Manifest." The six copies are routed as follows:

1. A copy is sent to the D.E.P.
2. A copy is sent to the state government of the generating facility such as New Jersey or Delaware if the disposal site is in PA.
3. A copy is signed by storage/disposal site and returned to the generating facility.
4. A copy is retained by the storage/disposal site.
5. A copy is retained by the transporter.
6. The original copy is retained by generator of the waste

In the event of contamination, the administrative authority such as the DEP will attempt to identify all those within the appropriate region who generate the substance or chemical agent causing the contamination. These generators might be required to submit copies of returned manifests along with additional information showing the amount of waste generated by each production process. Without the return copy, the company can be held as a PRP. The cost to the responsible parties or PRPs can be enormous. If ground water is contaminated, for example, the costs might include a new public water system for the affected area. Most matters are litigated, so resolution of the extent of the fines and remediation usually depend on a court order.

Waste disposal can also be a management letter item. Ideally, ways and means to reduce or eliminate waste should be sought for every waste-producing process. For example, substituting a less volatile chemical may increase chemical purchase costs but lower environmental risk and disposal costs. Such substitution is what the state of Pennsylvania calls a "source reduction strategy" or what accountants call an eco-audit. As another example, trucks now cleaned with a solvent-based cleaner can be cleaned with a citric-based cleaner that requires fewer disposal costs and less record keeping. A source reduction strategy might provide incentive for a company to hire a health and safety officer or an environmental hygienist to begin the process. In the long run, the cost savings could be significant

III. Guidance from the FASB, SFAS 5 and Statement of Position 96-1.[10]

In accounting for remediation, uncertainty reigns supreme! All of the parties associated with an environmental problem could potentially be liable for the cost of the cleanup-even if their contribution to the problem was very small. Before accepting significant financial responsibility, a company will negotiate, and-- depending on the amount--pursue a legal defense over the allocation of the cost between the involved parties. This is the first major uncertainty. The second major uncertainty is the actual cost of the cleanup. Preliminary remediation studies can yield vastly different results. The cost of the clean up will not be known with any degree of certainty until a detailed site remediation plan can actually assess the extent of the damage.

As a result of the financial uncertainty and prolonged negotiations, most companies will resist recording a financial liability even when named as a responsible party for fear that it will show an acknowledgement of guilt. Accounting rules support this position as long as particular uncertainties exist. Statement of Position 96-1[11] and SFAS 5 require that an obligation be reported when the following conditions are met:

1. A company has been identified as a potentially responsible party.

2. The company is participating in a remedial feasibility study.

3. A remedial feasibility study has been completed.

4. The cleanup method has been decided and cleanup costs have been estimated.

5. The firm has been ordered to clean up a site.

The auditor is faced with a conflict between full disclosure, FASB guidance and the goals of management. Certainly the allocation of cost uncertainty, litigation and negotiation concerns will dominate the disclosure conversation between management and the auditor.[12] This is another area that requires risk management by the auditor.

IV. Journal Entries and ABC.

In most situations, there are four levels of environmental costs that are important from an accounting perspective:[13]
Usual Costs of Operation such as disposal costs, which perhaps are not recognized but should be recognized. Hidden Regulatory Costs inclusive of reporting, permitting, monitoring, testing, training and inspection.[14] Contingent Liability Costs inclusive of penalties and fines for noncompliance, legal fees and settlement amounts for remedial actions, personal injuries and property damage.

4. A cost savings also might be realized from lower marketing costs as a result of increased consumer demand for environmentally friendly products, improved consumer satisfaction, improved employee relations and improved corporate image.

The major issue from a cost-control perspective is the proper allocation of costs to activities and then to products. Operations, which produce products and use Activity- Based Costing (ABC), will be more likely to attempt to properly allocate environmental costs to the products that cause environmental problems.

From an audit perspective, it is the lack of awareness and/or estimation of costs that generates audit risk. Most states keep extensive records of historical violations per generator. Auditors would be well advised to check state records when auditing a client with known violations or discharge areas on the site. In Pennsylvania the auditor should check: www.dep.state.pa.us, Subjects, eFacts, and then perform a search under the eFacts database.

V. A Christian Perspective

Where should Christians stand on environmental issues? Certainly the Scriptures are clear that the universe and everything in it belongs to God. The Scriptures also teach that we are accountable to God for being stewards of His creation (Genesis 1:27-28). And God promises, "I will send you rain in its season, and the ground will yield its crops and the trees of the field their fruit…" (Leviticus 26:4-5, New International Version).

What has emerged in the environmental debate is the age-old problem of confusing the order of creation with God Himself. From the beginning of time, mankind has falsely assigned god-like qualities to nonspiritual objects and then worshiped them as gods. The term "mother nature" refers to the complex ecosystems created by God to maintain order and balance on the earth. This is similar to the concept of giving "good luck" the credit for blessings instead of recognizing God's providence at work in our lives. Unfortunately, for many individuals "mother nature" has become the same as God and has become the source of all values. To these individuals, man is the intruder. Environmental decisions are made only in terms of what is best for nature.

Some members of the religious community have responded to the idolatry of making "mother nature" a god and other misperceptions with a doctrinal statement called the "Cornwall Declaration on Environmental Stewardship." The statement received its name from West Cornwall, Connecticut, where leading scholars from the Jewish, Catholic and Protestant community came together in October 1999 to craft an interfaith statement of common concerns and beliefs regarding environmental stewardship. Their statement can be found at .

Not far from West Cornwall, Connecticut, is the coastal town of Mystic, Connecticut, which illustrates the environmental debate. The town is a working model of a recreated 17th-century whaling community. The curators of Mystic describe in detail the risks and rewards of hunting and killing whales for their blubber, which was turned into oil for lamps. In hunting whales, harpoons were attached with rope to a small boat. When the hunters harpooned a whale, the whale towed the boat until the whale was exhausted. At the end of ride, the whale was butchered for its fat. Many sailors and many whales lost their lives on the "Nantucket slay ride." Why? Because from whales, humans wanted a product that advanced the human condition and economic progress.

Here is the dilemma. In the name of economic progress and an increased standard of living, the environment is destroyed. But the advancements from economic progress often can solve environmental problems just as the light bulb and electric power ended the slaughter of whales for their fat. Man is a consumer of the environment, but is simultaneously a creator who adds to the earth's abundance. What gift of new technology will God give to us to solve our fossil fuel shortage? Will God send oblivion to the human race by ultraviolet radiation penetrating through a hole in the ozone layer, or will He send deliverance in the form of a new technology? Not very many years ago, scientists predicted that everyone in northern climates would freeze to death for the lack of coal or firewood. Since the fall of Adam and Eve, humankind—whether individuals acknowledge it or not—has always been dependent upon God for deliverance from ourselves.

Is the environmental crisis real? Yes, it is real! The largest life forms on planet earth live in the rainforests of the Hoh River Valley in Washington's Olympic National Park. It takes five people touching hands to circle the base of one tree. Standing three hundred feet tall, these trees began life at about the time Jesus was born. Virgin forests were common in the United States and around the world about 1000 years ago. Not today. The virgin forests from Maine to North Carolina and west to the Mississippi have been reduced by 98%. The destruction of virgin forests worldwide constitutes a major environmental disaster in terms of clean water; clear air; flood control; and healthy, diverse ecosystems. In Haiti, for example, most of the forests have been consumed. Now each rainy season, more and more tillable soil washes off the rocks and out into the ocean. For the poor, there is no wood for fuel to cook food and no clean, uncontaminated water. The situation is grim and getting worse. Replacement forests, if we had room for them, would for many years lack the ability to retain soil, produce oxygen and function as watersheds. New York City, for example, depends on the watershed of the Catskill Mountains for clean water. Destroy the forests of the Catskills, and spend billions of dollars to provide NYC with clean water. Lost forests are only one example of the environmental crisis.

What are the solutions? Some believe it is the United Nations' responsibility to form a sort of international environmental protection agency. Most noteworthy was the United Nations Convention on Climate Change and the Kyoto Protocol Treaty, which is facing consideration by 150 industrial nations. The treaty would regulate the reduction of "man-made greenhouse gases in the atmosphere, such as carbon dioxide, by a total of about 5% overall—based on 1990 levels—between 2008 and 2012." In the U.S., for example, the Kyoto Protocol Treaty calls for a reduction of 7%, and critics estimate the cost to the U.S. at $300 billion per year. The treaty would impact every industry that burns fuels. Of course, this depends on ratification and funding by Congress, and the treaty certainly has many opponents. Copies of the treaty, including background information, are available at . The official United Nations' site is .

Other preservationists believe ecotourism is part of the answer. Charging tourists to visit and play in the natural ecosystems is saving some natural areas. It has worked well for Costa Rica and Puerto Rico. Some nations use the resulting funds to retire the national debt at reduced rates in return for preserving natural areas.

Dozens of other ideas exist. The solutions are a matter of perspective. All of us who live, eat and breathe on this planet need to respect it. We need to see it as a part of our future. We need to see the interdependence of the biosphere. We need to recognize our responsibility for the stewardship of God's creation. In all of these perspectives, Christians should take the lead, working as if it depends on our actions and praying as if it depends on God's grace for new technologies.

Table I. Types of Disposable Waste

Residual waste: non hazardous waste created by a process

Municipal waste: household waste, C & D waste and infectious waste

Hazardous waste: Listed in Title 40 – Protection of the Environment, (C.F.R.), EPA, Chapter 1, section 261.31 & 32 (PA, for example, has adopted the federal regulation for the definition of hazardous waste. Some states have taken a more stringent approach.) There are basically four characteristics of substances that qualify them as hazardous waste:

1. Ignitability: Wastes that can readily catch fire and sustain combustion such as paints and cleaners.
2. Corrosivity: Wastes that are acidic or alkaline such as sulfuric acid from automotive batteries.
3. Reactivity: Wastes that readily explode or undergo violent reactions such as discarded munitions or explosives.
4. Toxicity: Wastes that leach dangerous concentrations of toxic chemicals into the ground water.

Table II. Reference Materials

Measuring Corporate Environmental Performance: Best Practices for Costing and Measuring an Effective Environmental Strategy. By Marc J. Epstein, Ph.D. Co-published by Irwin and the Institute of Management Accountants Foundation for Applied Research, 1997.

Advances in Environmental Accounting & Management. Edited by Martin Freedman and Bikki Jaggi. Published by an imprint of Elsevier Science, 2000.

Environmental Disclosure: When and How to Disclose Environmental Matters Under SEC and Accounting Requirements. Published by Massachusetts Continuing Legal Education, 2000.

Contemporary Environmental Accounting Issues, Concepts and Practice. By Stefan Schaltegger and Roger Burritt. Published by Greenleaf Publishing, 2000. (This is a 462-page environmental accounting textbook.)

<u>Title 40 – Protection of the Environment, Chapter 1.</u> Known as "40 CFR." This Federal Law title details all the federal laws related to environmental protection. The major parts dealing with hazardous waste management and the functioning of the agency are parts 260 to 299. Like the Internal Revenue Code, this is a massive amount of material to read. Parts 260 to 265 are more than 500 pages long.

<u>RCRA Orientation Manual.</u> Published by the EPA. The EPA says the manual "has proven to be a popular and valuable resource for anyone working with the EPA's solid and hazardous waste." Available from the U.S. Environmental Protection Agency, Office of Solid Waste/Communications, Information, and Resources Management Division, 401 M Street, SW, Washington, D.C. 20460.

<u>Pennsylvania Code, Title 25. Environmental Protection, Department of Environmental Protection.</u> This is *the* major source of environmental law in Pennsylvania. Residual Waste Management is covered in one book from chapters 287 through 299. Municipal Waste Management is dealt with in chapters 271 through 285 and is covered in another book. Each chapter is about 100 pages long and is significantly more readable than federal code sections. Available from the Department of Environmental Protection, Bureau of Land Recycling and Waste Management, Division of Municipal and Residual Waste, Rachel Carson State Office Building, 14th floor, 400 Market Street, Harrisburg, PA 17105-8472. Phone: (717) 787-7381. Each of the code books will list a date for which it is current through a certain Pennsylvania Bulletin (Pa. B.). Similar to federal publications such as *The Cumulative Bulletin* of the federal government, readers must consult the Pa. B. for the current law. The Pa. B. is available from Fry Communications Inc., 800 W. Church Rd., Mechanicsburg, PA 17055-3198. For example, Pa. B. Vol. 29, Number 18, provides an update on the Environmental Quality Board's hazardous waste regulation. Most regulations are also available from the DEP web site. Under subjects, go to "land recycling" and then "EFACTS."

<u>Hazardous Waste Management.</u> By Michael D. LaGrega, Phillip Buckingham & Jeffrey C. Evans. Published by McGraw Hill Inc.,

1994. In more than 1000 pages, the authors examine current management practices, treatment and disposal methods, as well as site remediation. The book is highly recommended as the leader in the field.

[1] Jonathan E. Bower is a Waste Management Specialist in the Waste Management Program of the Pennsylvania Department of Environmental Protection (DEP). Opinions and interpretations expressed in this article regarding environmental laws do not necessarily represent DEP's position on the law or enforcement of the law and should not be taken as a substitute for directly contacting DEP with questions and concerns. The DEP Southeast Regional Office is located at Lee Park, 555 North Lane, Conshohocken, PA 19428.

1 Costanza, Robert, Ecological Economics: The Science and Management of Sustainability, Columbia U.
           Press, N.Y. 1991

[2] In 1980 the Comprehensive Environmental Response, Compensation, and Liability Act (CERCLA) was passed by the U.S. Congress. The legislation authorized the federal government to hold polluters financially responsible for cleanup costs.

[3] Andrews, Andrea; Simonetti, Gilbert, *Litigation/Management Accounting: Tort Reform Revolution.* A.I.C.P.A., Journal of Accountancy, September 1996, 9-96 J.A. 53. Also see, *Accountants Liability,* Practicing Law Institute, 1:2 Services Commonly Performed by Accountants & Chapter 2, Standards of the Accounting Profession, Copyright 2001.

[4] Full Cost Accounting in Action: Case Studies of Six Solid Waste Management Agencies, EPA, Solid Waste and Emergency Response, December 1998.

[5] General Procedures, Program aam54020.pgm, Copyright 1996 A.I.C.P.A. Inc.

[6] General Procedures, Audit Objectives, Practitioners Clearing House, Fort Worth, TX, Feb. 2000.

[7] Sunoco, Inc., *1999 Health and Environment & Safety Review and CERES Report.* Page 44. For more information on CERES (Coalition for Environmentally Responsible Economics) go to http://www.ceres.org
 ISO 14000 Info Center: www.iso14000.com.
 Rezaee, Z. Help Keep the World Green, *Journal of Accountancy*, November 2000, #57.

[8] Cox, Robert M. Jr., *Tough Environmental Regulations Bring New Opportunities for CPA's,* Pennsylvania CPA Journal, Summer 2001.
 Willits, S. D., and Metil, M. G. "Eco-audits examine operations to find ways to avoid environmental problems and to conserve resources." In, "Roles for CPA's in Clients' Eco-Audits," *Pennsylvania CPA Journal*, December 1996.

[9] Klavens, Jonathan S. Esq., Chair; Clack, Holly A. CPA; Koch, Gayle CPA; McCaffery Maura; Newell, John O. Esq., <u>Environmental Disclosure, When and How to Disclose Environmental Matters Under SEC and Accounting Requirements,</u> Massachusetts Continuing Legal Education, Inc. 2000.

[10] Trott, Edward., Chair of the Environmental Accounting Task Force said the SOP has omitted a discussion of the measurement of the legal cost of the remediation liability, "from the comment letters this was the most contentious issue." Journal of Accounting, October 1996, page 17.

[11] Mary E. Barth, Maureen F. McNichols, and G. Peter Wilson, 1997, "Factors Influencing Firms' Disclosure about Environmental Liabilities," Review of Accounting Studies 2, (1):35-64.

[12] Bailey, Paul. *Full Cost Accounting for Life-Cycle Costs – A Guide for Engineers and Financial Analysts,* Environmental Finance, spring 1991.

[13] Kreuze, Jerry G. CPA and Newell, Gale, CMA, *ABC and Life-Cycle Costing for Environmental Expenditures,* Management Accounting, February 1994, 38 to 42.
Dappern, A., and Johnson, R. 2000, Dec. Taking a stand. *Hemispheres*: 107.
Sauer, L. J. 1998. *The Once and Future Forest.* Washington, D.C.: Island Press.
The United Nations has a problem getting consensus on environmental issues. For example, the "Report by the Expert Working Group Meeting on Improving Governments' Role in the Promotion of Environmental Managerial Accounting" reports, "There is no consensus on the scope, content, or procedures of Environmental Managerial Accounting" (Division for Sustainable Development, 2000).
Fialka, J. J. 2000, Nov. 27. "Climate talks are suspended amid deadlock." Wall Street Journal: A3.
The Global Climate Coalition (an industry PAC) offers a critical view of the Kyoto Protocol Treaty. For articles explaining opposition to the treaty, see the *Chemical Week* Web site or *The American City Business Journals Inc.*
The Kyoto Protocol Treaty is available to the public by contacting the National Council for Science and the Environment, 1725 K Street, NW, Suite 212, Washington, D.C. 20006. Phone number: (202) 530-5810.
EPA. <u>RCRA Orientation Manual.</u>
The Resource Conservation and Recovery Act (RCRA) was enacted in 1976 to address the huge volumes of municipal and industrial solid waste generated nationwide. The act also governs the management of underground storage tanks.

Part IV

Accounting and Moral Philosophy

THE INTEGRATION OF FAITH, REASON & JUSTICE,
Faculty Goals & Objectives

By
Dr. Jack E. Bower
Eastern University

Business Professors are sometimes confronted with questions like, "How can you be a Christian and teach business?" Unfortunately, students sometimes equate business enterprise with worldliness and the love of money. The truth is that in a business context **knowledge is power.** Therefore business education is about empowerment. Empowered to serve God and others by increasing ones capacity for service. Empowered to realize one's full potential by being challenged to think and respond in totally new ways. Our goal as Christian business faculty is that our graduates are empowered to know what is just, to make the right decisions and use this knowledge for good instead of evil.

A good place to begin a business class is with a reading from Luke 16:1-13. It is a parable about management of accounts receivable. The story ends with this line; *"So if you have not been trustworthy in handling worldly wealth, who will trust you with true riches?"* Jesus is very clear in saying that the proper management of worldly wealth is a prerequisite to being trusted with spiritual wealth. The study of business can make you a more trustworthy steward of God's gifts to each of us and of His universe, if you seek to serve Him.

"Teachers can teach much more than their subject matter and much more than styles of thinking. They teach ethics and values and purpose and determination even while they are also teaching Finance 101. Teaching is a total process. While the finance may be taught analytically, those other things are being taught at the same time by selectively reinforcing, punishing, ignoring, and encouraging students. For the learner, everything in the teacher-learner situation is part of the educational process. In the classroom, students learn from the passion as well as the analytic virtuosity of their professors. They listen to integrity as well as brilliance, to determination as well as content..." [1]

The primary goal of Christian business faculty is to mentor all of the students on their spiritual journey in a right relationship with God. Their task is to encourage spiritual formation within the church and academic community. Christian faculty will take the time to listen to the heart of each student and to make the time together a nurturing relationship.[2] Dr. Modica, the chaplain at Eastern College, calls this a transformational relationship instead of a transactional one. Faculty try to be critical without being cynical.[3] Christian faculty will try to convey a message of hope even if you are failing in a course.[4] Each professor struggles every day to search for that teachable moment when your heart is open to hearing the truth. May God give each of us, teachers and students alike, the wisdom, humility and courage to be in nurturing relationships.

The secondary goal of Christian business faculty is to help you integrate your faith into your professional and personal life.[5] For business students this means your faith must impact daily decision-making. Dr. Howard, the Provost at Eastern College, describes life as a laboratory for testing our faith. He believes that there is no separation between the sacred and the secular, work is in fact worship.[6] The Business faculty wholeheartedly agrees with and practice this perspective.

Our total lives should be given to the glory of God. This means integrating our Christian values into the corporate environment where competition often demands taking a hard line.[7] Today, more than ever, Christian business educators need to train and graduate students who are not only competent in business skills but who also have a strong conscience.[8] Love your neighbor as yourself is a universal principle. Helping you to develop a strong conscience for right decision making is one of our most challenging tasks. We must continue to force you to think about complex justice issues[9] Decisions made in the classroom over cases on ethics can have a significant impact on the real situations faced daily in life.[10]

Integration of faith and learning means that you will walk with God and show love toward others as outlined briefly in the above paragraphs.[11] These are, in fact, the greatest of the commandments (Matt. 22:37-40). Professors like to reason from the general to the specific. The following are five specific business objectives (Christ like perspectives) that we try to instill in all of our students. The ordering is not significant because the needs are different for each student:

obedient

#1 Experience Life, be a risk taker: My parents were fond of saying that people who never make any mistakes are people who never do anything. *"Experience is the school of life. We are not confronted with clear propositions to be accepted or rejected, but with complicated situations within which we must learn."*[12] Doing something is usually better than doing nothing; perfectionism can lead to procrastination or inactivity.[13]

We operate in an extremely complex economy. Students often need help in breaking down complex tasks into steps that can be accomplished one at a time. Accounting and finance professors, for example, focused their teaching energies on making the complex financial world understandable and entertaining to students.[14] Dr. Campolo is fond of saying that *education is entertainment with a purpose.*

Risk taking, one step at a time, is a valuable lesson for success in the business world. Even in the spiritual world we need to be risk takers. Jesus said, *"Whoever finds his life will lose it, and whoever loses his life for my sake will find it"*(Matt. 10:39). Whether in following Jesus or in business decision-making, we all need to take risks. We have only to study the heroes of the Bible to see risk takers, from the Patriarch to Jesus. Great things were accomplished by risk takers acting one step at a time. Jesus told a parable about a wealthy landowner who gave management of his vineyard to a certain group of evil managers. The landowner sent auditors to the vineyard who were ignored or mistreated. In the end, he sent his son who was killed. Jesus was a risk taker in coming to earth to die for our sins.[15] The servant who had the one mina *"laid it away in a piece of cloth"* was rebuked by Jesus for not taking the risk of investing the money with the moneychangers. When David heard Goliath boasting, he said, why not send me. Some of the most successful entrepreneurs are so because they are risk takers.

Risk taking is of particular interest when teaching finance where the class spends a considerable amount of time on financial markets and risk. In this setting, you are encouraged to dream and contemplate the risks and rewards of financial management. Walking with God also has its risks and rewards. Certainly you need to see people in various walks of life and say, why not me? I could do that someday!

Risk takers also know how to make a break with their past. Paul participated in the stoning of Stephen, yet he didn't let this keep him from looking towards the future. *"Forgetting what is behind and straining towards the goal to win the prize for which God has called me heavenward in Christ Jesus"* (Phil 3:13). You will be encouraged to strain toward the goal, to win the prize. Many people are afraid of the future; they back away from it and live in the past.[16] Christians should be straining forward ready for new challenges and new opportunities, "to take full advantage of this present; to live this day as if it were our last, as if we were going to die as martyrs at the end of the day,"[17] Risk takers are the salt and light spoken of in Matt. 5:13. In a recent newspaper comic strip, the punch line read like this, *"Yep life sure is a great gift, but I guess there's always going to be those content to play with just the box."*[18] I like the quote from Dr. Campolo; *"I try to help young people see them-selves as agents of God, commissioned to a vocation of ultimate importance. With this understanding, they'll have a sense of calling that generates unparalleled enthusiasm for life."*[19]

<u>#2 Have a sense of destiny and a sense of God's protection:</u> Jesus said, *"You have no power over me unless it was given to you from on high"* (John 19:11). Luke said, God has *"determined the times set for them and the exact places where they should live"* (Acts 17:26). You need to seek God's will for your life.[20] You need to know that if you are seeking Him, your next job or next project is a part of God's purpose for your life.[21] When faced with a tough decision we all need to remember to pray about it, asking God to reveal his will to us so that we choose the correct path.[22] You will find that the business faculty believe that God has a plan for their lives and that in being at Eastern they are doing what He has called them to do.[23] You should learn to feel a sense of destiny in your professional as well as personal life.[24]

Destiny, like most spiritual gifts, is a magnet that pulls us closer to God.[25] The hard part is knowing when opposition to our plans is God trying to show us another road or is He testing us.[26] We certainly don't want to ignore God's messages. Giving Him the credit in every situation is a key to joyful living. So many people feel distant from God when problems enter their lives.[27] The truth is that these may be the moments when they could be the closest to God.[28] It can sometimes be very difficult to see the leading of God in your life and to learn from an unpleasant experience.[29]

#3 Submit to authorities: For business students paying taxes and obeying the laws of the government are major issues.[30] We all must learn to show respect to government officials as opposed to resenting their intrusions into our lives.[31] It is interesting to note that the early debates over the constitutionality of the income tax concerned the government knowing this type of personal information.[32]

The function of government is to "prolong and protect" our precious moments here on earth.[33] If you major in accounting, you will spend a considerable amount of time discussing attitudes about paying taxes. We have clear direction from God to pay our taxes (Romans 13: 6ff) & (Matt. 22:15ff).[34] Unfortunately, the world creates a different expectation in the minds of students where profit comes from the victimization of other taxpayers.[35] Any accountant who is a Christian can tell story upon story of people who seek to deceive the IRS on their tax returns including many Christian nonprofit organizations. God does not favor those who practice rebellion and deceitfulness.[36]

On the other hand, this does not mean that we should not work to correct problems in our society not being addressed by the government or that we should not seek to change our government.[37] It is important to learn to be good citizens, to exercise your right to vote and to hold elected officials accountable for the decisions they make.[38] Some of the best discussions in class have followed chapel speeches by Christians immersed in the world's moral problems. These are critical issues for discussion and a part of the integration of faith and learning.

It's not the amount of money that determines materialism.

#4 Avoid being seduced by materialism: Satan says, "He who dies with the most toys wins!" Jesus says, *"A man's life does not consist in the abundance of his possessions"* (Luke 12:13-21). One of our great struggles as Christians is not to be seduced by the world into defining success in Satan's terms.[39] The world says it is what you do as a profession or your physical appearance that defines your self worth. Christians should resent both of these perspectives. It is our relationship to God through His Son that defines who we are. There is a self-confidence that comes from being a child of God. Mankind looks on the outside but God sees on the inside (Mark 2:8). Our goal is to have His eyes, to see the pure heart and Godlike qualities in everyone. Yet, at the same time we have to be trained to recognize evil and avoid it. Bringing a discussion about the love of money or preoccupation with acquiring wealth into the classroom can be difficult.[40] Students generally do not like to talk about it unless encouraged to do so.[41]

We have to create a sensitivity for the needy of this world as we grow in our love of God and neighbors.[42] You must see success in terms of the positive impact you have had on others and in terms of the people you have trained to carry on after you are gone. Like Paul, we should learn to be content whatever the circumstances. *"I know what it is to be content in any and every situation, whether well fed or hungry, whether living in plenty or in want. I can do everything through him who gives me strength"* (Phil 4:12,13).

#5 Keep your work in the proper perspective: We serve a working God. His work is great, awesome and marvelous. Because we are made in the image of God, we also should be creatures of work. Work provides the income that buys food, clothing and shelter and the opportunities to share with others. God speaks out against laziness in II Thessalonians 3:6ff. *"And whatever you do, whether in word or deed, do it all in the name of the Lord Jesus Christ, giving thanks to God the Father through him"* (Col. 3:17).

There has been significant criticism of the "Protestant work ethic." Certainly when taken to extremes, work can be destructive. If too much time is given to the job and therefore family or the church community is neglected, it is a problem.[43] The Christian work ethic is not dead. You will be encouraged to perform intense and diligent work while in college and after graduation. Hopefully, you will have a balanced perspective so that you can make the proper choices between work and family.[44] "For God did not give us a spirit of timidity, but a spirit of power, of love and of self-discipline."[45]

The work issue is critical for accounting majors where many

public accounting firms ask employees to work 60 hours per week during the tax and audit season. Release time is then given during the summer and fall. Phil Zink, a former accounting professor at Eastern College, liked to say that you cannot get sick, fall in love, or get married during tax season. The message from accounting alumni is always the same. Be prepared for long hours during the audit and tax season.

SUMMARY

If we as Christian business faculty have motivated you to have the courage to take risks, have a sense of purpose, show the proper respect for authority, not to be lovers of money and know how to keep life's choices in perspective; then we have been successful in our endeavor as teachers.[46] While holding students in the highest regard, we truly want to call you to a Godly standard.[47] This is the integration of faith, reason and justice and is our purpose as faculty for being here at this place and time.

BIBLIOGRAPHY

Bondi, Roberta C. To Love as God Loves.
    Philadelphia: Fortress Press, 1987.

Borsch, Frederick H. God's Parable. Philadelphia:
    The Westminster Press, 1975.

Bowden, John, and James Richmond, ed. A Reader in
    Contemporary Theology. Philadelphia: The Westminster
Press, 1967.

Bruce, F. F. The Tyndale New Testament
    Commentaries. Grand Rapids: William B. Eerdmans
    Publishing Company, 1969.

Byrne, H. W. A Christian Approach to Education.
    Grand Rapids: Zondervan Publishing House, 1961.

Carey, George. Why I Believe in a Personal God.
        Wheaton: Harold Shaw Publishers, 1989.

Ditmanson, Harold H., Howard V. Hong, and Warren A.
        Quanbeck, eds. Christian Faith and the Liberal Arts.
        Minneapolis: Augsburg Publishing House, 1960.

Donceel, Joseph F. The Searching Mind. London:
        University of Notre Dame Press, 1979.

Ferre, Nels F. S. Christian Faith and Higher Education.
        New York: Harper & Brothers, 1954.

Ferre, Nels F. S. Reason in Religion. London: Thomas
        Nelson and Sons LTD, 1963.

Ficken, Clarence E. Building a Faculty. Nashville:
        Board of Education of The   Methodist Church, 1956.

Fisher, Fred L. The Purpose of God and the Christian
        Life. Philadelphia: The Westminster Press, 1952.

Foster, Richard J. Prayer. San Francisco: Harper
        Collins, 1964.

Fowler, James W. Becoming Adult, Becoming Christian.
        San Francisco: Harper & Row, 1984.

Fowler, James W., and Sam Keen. Life Maps. Waco:
        Word Books, 1978.

Galilea, Segundo, trans. Spirituality of Hope. Maryknoll:
        Orbis Books, 1989.

Holloway, Richard. Crossfire: Faith and Doubt in an
        Age of Certainty. Grand Rapids: William B. Eerdmans
        Publishing Company, 1988.

Jones, Laurie Beth. <u>Jesus, CEO</u>. New York: Hyperion,
	1995.

Kennedy, Eugene C. <u>Believing</u>. Garden City:
	Doubleday &Company, 1974.

LeFevre, Perry. <u>The Christian Teacher</u>. New York:
	Abingdon Press, MCMLVIII.

Lewis, C. S. <u>Beyond Personality</u>. New York: The
	Macmillan Company, 1947.

Mackenzie, Donald M., and Manning M. Pattillo.
	<u>Church-Sponsored Higher Education
	in the United States</u>. Washington: American Council
	on Education, 1966.

Marstin, Ronald. <u>Beyond Our Tribal Gods</u>. Maryknoll:
	Orbis Books, 1979.

McKeachie, Wilbert J. <u>New Directions for Teaching and
	Learning</u>. San Francisco: Jossey-Bass Inc., 1980

Morris, William H., ed. <u>Effective College Teaching</u>.
	Washington: American Council on Education, 1970.

Newbigin, Lesslie. <u>Proper Confidence</u>. Grand Rapids:
	William B. Eerdmans Publishing Company, 1995.

Newell, William R. <u>Romans</u>. Chicago: Moody Press,
	1938.

Pace, C. Robert. <u>Education and Evangelism</u>. New
	York: McGraw-Hill Book Company, 1972.

Parsonage, Robert R., ed. <u>Church Related Higher
	Education</u>. Valley Forge: Judson Press, 1978.

Pelikan, Jaroslav J., and others. <u>Religion and the
    University</u>. Canada: University of Toronto Press, 1964.

Phenix, Philip H. <u>Education and the Worship of God</u>.
    Philadelphia: The Westminster Press, MCMLXVI.

Phillips, J. B. <u>Your God is Too Small</u>. New York: The
    MacMillan Company, 1958.

Pullias, Earl V., and others. <u>Toward Excellence in
    College Teaching</u>. Dubuque: William C. Brown Company,
1963.

Ramm, Bernard. <u>The Christian College in the Twentieth
    Century</u>. Grand Rapids: William B. Eerdmans Publishing
    Company, 1963.

Roberts, Oral. <u>Miracle of Seed-Faith</u>. Tulsa: Fleming
    H. Revell Company, 1970.

Robertson, Roland, ed. <u>Sociology of Religion</u>.
    Baltimore: Penguin Books, 1969.

Scharf, Betty R. <u>The Sociological Study of Religion</u>.
    New York: Harper & Row,   1970.

Schuller, Robert H. <u>Tough Minded Faith for Tender
    Hearted People</u>. Nashville: Thomas Nelson Publishers, 1983.

Thiessen, Elmer J. <u>Teaching for Commitment</u>. London:
    McGill-Queen's University Press, 1993.

Thomas, J. D. <u>The Spirit and Spirituality</u>. Abilene:
    Biblical Research Press, 1966.

Trueblood, Elton. <u>A Place to Stand</u>. New York:
    Harper & Row, 1969.

Von Grueningen, John Paul, ed. <u>Toward a Christian Philosophy of Higher Education</u>. Philadelphia: The Westminster Press, MCMLVII.

Woodyard, David O. <u>Beyond Cynicism</u>. Philadelphia: Westminster Press, MCMLXXII.

[1] Leavitt, Harold J., <u>Corporate Pathfinders</u>, pp 96-97 (from faculty handbook).

[2] Pullias, Earl V., and others, <u>Towards Excellence in College Teaching</u>, (Dubuque: William C. Brown Co., 1963), page 35.

[3] Woodyard, David O., <u>Beyond Cynicism</u>, (Philadelphia: Westminster Press, MCMLXXII).

[4] Morris, William H., ed., <u>Effective College Teaching</u>, (Washington: American Council on Education, 1970), page 120.

[5] Ditmanson, Harold H., Howard V. Hong, and Warren A Quanbeck, eds., <u>Christian Faith and the Liberal Arts</u>, (Minneapolis: Augsburg Publishing House, 1960.), page 76.
Ferre, Nels F. S. <u>Christian Faith and Higher Education</u>, (New York: Harper & Brothers, 1954), page 28 on practical and professional capacities.

[6] The speech was given on 4/21/96 to the graduate student worship assembly. This speech by Dr. Howard and our conversation afterwards had a major influence on the outline of this paper.

[7] Holloway, Richard, <u>Crossfire: Faith and Doubt in an Age of Certainty</u>, (Grand Rapids: William E. Eerdmans Publishing Co., 1988), page 36.

[8] Phenix, Philip H., <u>Education and the Worship of God</u>, (Philadelphia: Westminster Press, MCMLXVI), page 115.

[9] Pelikan, Jaroslav J., and others, <u>Religion and the University</u>, (Canada: University of Toronto Press, 1964), page 121.

[10] McKeachie, Wilbert J., <u>New Directions for Teaching and Learning</u>, (San Francisco: Jossey-Bass Inc. 1980), page 44, "Learning from Prototype Models".

[11] Bondi, Robert C., <u>To Love as God Loves</u>, (Philadelphia: Fortress Press, 1987), page 20.

[12] Ferre, Nels F.S., <u>Christian Faith and Higher Education</u>, (New York: Harper & Brothers, 1954), page 78.

[13] Phillips, J.B., <u>Your God is too Small</u>, (The MacMillan Company-New York), page 28.

[14] Fowler, James W., <u>Becoming Adult, Becoming Christian</u>, (San Francisco: Harper & Row, 1984), page 95.

[15] Philippians 2:6ff.

[16] Woodyard, David O., Beyond Cynicism, (Philadelphia: Westminster Press, MCMLXXII), page 55 "The Power of the Future."

[17] Galilea, Segundo, Spirituality of Hope, (Maryknoll: Orbis Books, 1978), page 62.

[18] Phila. Inquirer, Bent Halos.

[19] MacTavish, Stephanie, A Joyful Community, Living the Life of Faith at Eastern College, 1996.

[20] Romans 8:12ff.

[21] Roberts, Oral., Miracle of Seed-Faith, (Tulsa: Fleming H Revell Co., 1970).

[22] Trueblood, Elton, A Place to Stand, (Harper & Row, Publishers, 1969), page 82, The Reality of Prayer.
(I often mention this book in class when talking about net present value; NPV is the place to stand in finance just like the resurrection is the place to stand for Christians).

[23] Fisher, Fred, The Purpose of God and the Christian Life, (Westminster Press, Philadelphia, MCMLXII), page 113.

[24] I like the explanation of Calvinism often given by Dr. Miles. "When we get to heaven and walk through the arch it will say *for whosoever will.* When we have passed through the arch and look back, it will say *predestined from the foundations of the world.*

[25] James 1:2ff and II Corinthians 5:1ff.

[26] Jones, Laurie Beth, Jesus, CEO (Chief Executive Officer), (New York:Hyperion, 1995). This is a devotional book that I often use in my accounting class because of her keen insights into the leadership style of Jesus.

[27] Carey, George, "Archbishop of Canterbury", Why I Believe in a Personal God, (Harold Shaw Publishers, Wheaton, Il.), "Good, Evil and God", page 73.

[28] Kennedy, Eugene C., Believing, (Garden City: Doubleday & Company, 1974), page 64.

[29] Foster, Richard J., Prayer, (San Francisco: Harper Collins, 1964), page 23.

[30] Scharf, Betty R. The Sociological Study of Religion, (Harper Torchbooks, London, 1970). Dr. Scharf is a lecturer in Sociology in the London School of Economics. This text and others suggest that religion was created and is maintained by governments to keep its citizens in submission to authority.

[31] Romans 13:2ff.

[32] Hoffman, Smith, Willis, Individual Income Taxes, (West's Federal Taxation, 1996 edition, Eagan, MN), Chapter One.

[33] Lewis, C.S., Beyond Personality, (The MacMillian Co., N.Y., 1947), page 43.

[34] Newell, William R., Romans Verse by Verse, (Moody Press, Chicago, 1938).

[35] Borsch, Frederick Houk, God's Parable, (The Westminster Press, Phila, 1975), page 72, Acts of Power.

[36] Romans 13:2.

[37] Trueblood, D. Elton, The Marks of a Christian College, (Found in *Towards a Christian Philosophy of Higher Education,* John Paul von Grueningen Editor, The Westminster Press, Phila, MCMLVII), page 161.

[38] Ramm, Bernard, The Christian College in the Twentieth Century, (William B. Eerdmans Publishing Co. Grand Rapids, Michigan), page 64.

[39] Fowler, James W., and Sam Keen., Life Maps, (Waco: Word Books, 1978), page 109.

[40] Marstin, Ronald., Beyond Our Tribal Gods, "The Maturing of Faith", (Orbis Books, Maryknoll, N.Y. 1982), page 125, "Wealth and the Gospel".

[41] I have read several books on "Christian Financial Concepts" by Larry Burket and I often use his techniques in class. I have also taught workshops in churches using books and tapes published by his organization.

[42] Eastern College Mission Statement.

[43] Ferre, Nels F.S., Christian Faith and Higher Education, (New York: Harper & Brothers 1954), page 115

[44] Byrne, H.W., A Christian Approach to Education, (Zondervan Publishing House, Michigan, 1961), page 276. Dr. Byrne was Dean of Fort Worth Bible College. His book has an excellent list of learning objectives in many subject areas. The list for economics is well done.

[45] II Timothy 1:7.

[46] This is not intended as an all inclusive list. There are excellent lists in a book by C. Robert Pace, Education and Evangelism, (Carnegie Commission on Higher Education, McGraw-Hill Book Co., N.Y., 1972).

[47] Ficken, Charence E. Building a Faculty, (Nashville: Board of Education of the Methodist Church, 1956), page 29.

A Christian Perspective on Accounting: Making the Invisible Visible

By
Lynn Spellman White
Trinity Christian College

Introduction

This is a challenging time for the accounting profession. Public trust in the content of financial reports is eroding, largely from concern that companies are manipulating accounting procedures in order to improve financial results. Byrnes, Melcher, and Sparks (1998) suggest that some companies engage in earnings hocus-pocus by booking revenues too early and abusing restructuring charges. The ability of the discipline to attract the best and the brightest students to its study has come into question due to ever-increasing demands placed on students and competition from other fields of study. Also, accountants are struggling with the breadth of services demanded by clients and the resulting strain of maintaining an appropriate level of professional expertise in all requested areas (Thomas, 1998).

In response to these and other concerns, the American Institute of Certified Public Accountants (AICPA) is currently conducting CPA Vision Project Future Forums in an attempt to build consensus among accounting professionals regarding which professional services are important now and which services will be important to the future of the profession. The AICPA is also engaged in a public image campaign that is designed to highlight the strategic importance of accounting information to management decision-making as well as the broad range of services performed by accountants. The new chairperson of the AICPA, Stuart Kessler, has even suggested that one way to enhance the CPA image is to change what the letters stand for. He proposes calling CPAs "Certified Professional Advisers" because he believes the term more closely reflects the competencies that set the profession apart. Kessler states:

I would like to change *public* to *professional* because over 50% of our members work outside of public practice and the term is confusing. . . . I would replace *accountant* with *adviser*, because adviser conjures up a better image of what CPAs do for clients, and it's what will set us apart now and in the 21st century (Von Brachel, 1997, p. 71).

Presented with such a contentious environment, the accounting profession views the beginning of this millennium as a critical time in its professional development. As a result, the accounting profession is exhibiting a rather unusual willingness to examine and question the core values and assumptions upon which it is built. This situation creates tremendous opportunities for the Christian accountant. Now is the time for Christian accountants to encourage a vision of accounting that expands the traditional boundaries of the profession. This expansion, however, must not be fueled by the profession's self-serving desire to increase its power-base in society. Rather, the expansion needs to be a natural outgrowth of applying biblical principles to accounting. Harrison (1990) proposes that:

Biblical principles provide the ideal basis for identifying fairness in accounting. Outlined in sufficient detail to give workable guidelines and effected by the Holy Spirit, the principles provide insights into the very mind of the infinite personal God. With a God-centered world view, God's Word can be applied to all accounting determinations (p. 110).

Accounting and Servant Leadership

The ultimate goal of the accounting, or any other profession, must be to honor God in all its activities. Through Jesus' own example we see that honoring God involves sacrificial service to our fellow man. Page (1996) notes that it was in Jesus' washing of the feet of the disciples that we have the classic model [of servant leadership] for all time (pp. 68-69).

After he had washed their feet, had put on his robe, and had returned to the table, he said to them, "Do you know what I have done to you? You call me Teacher and Lord – and you are right, for that is what I am. So if I, your Lord and Teacher, have washed your feet, you also ought to wash one another's feet. For I have set you an example, that you also should do as I have done to you" (John 13:12-15).

A Christian Perspective on Accounting for Human Resources

The biblical principle of servant leadership has great significance to the accounting profession. By focusing the accounting profession's attention on service to society as opposed to increasing its own authority in society, the accounting profession would be moving closer to a biblically-informed approach to professionalism. For example, current accounting practices only provide the users of financial information with a vision of the cost dimension of Human Resource (HR) activities within an organization. However, for quite some time there have been utility models available that measure the full economic impact of HR activities, both costs and benefits (Boudreau, 1983, 1984; Boudreau & Berger, 1985). This information could prove to be useful to society since it might encourage organizations to invest more aggressively in their human capital and would also provide the public with more complete information to inform their investment decisions. The accounting profession has not embraced the concept of human resource accounting, stating that the models are impractical to implement (Roslender, 1992). In current practice, very few organizations employ utility models to measure the effectiveness of HR activities (Carnevale & Schulz, 1990), and it is unlikely that organizations will encourage the development of human resource accounting procedures for external reporting if they perceive it as expanding their scope of accountability. As Roslender notes, human resource accounting has an obvious potential for promoting accountability to the work force as an element of an employment report (p. 105).

While it is true that utility models require the use of statistical estimation techniques, the benefits they provide in the form of increased information on the utility of HR programs appears to exceed their costs. However, given the accounting profession's need to appear objective and precise, accountants seem to perceive utility models as a threat to the status of the accounting profession and therefore prioritize the self-interests of the profession over the interests of society.

This chapter will explore how examining accounting policy from a critical perspective expands one's ability to interpret and understand the current composition of accounting standards. Chua (1986) notes that:

> Within a critical perspective, the accounting profession is no longer theorized as a neutral group which evolves in response to rational demands for useful information. Instead, it is an aspiring occupational monopoly that seeks to further its own social and economic self-interest (p. 624).

Within the critical perspective, power theory can be used by Christian accountants to examine the underlying factors behind the current boundaries of accounting practice. These boundaries often seem to exist to support the accounting profession's desire for professional authority (one of the key attributes of a profession, Jones, 1995) as opposed to public concerns. The accounting profession's focus on maintaining its professional authority tends to encourage actions that are more similar to a domineering, selfish leadership style as opposed to a servant leadership style. Page (1996) refers to these conflicting approaches to leadership at the individual level, but they also serve to inform the discussion of leadership at the level of the profession. By departing from a traditional functionalist perspective on professionalism, the Christian accountant is freed from the controlling nature of accounting's status quo and can be encouraged to seek ways in which biblical principles can be applied to accounting information.

Current Christian Scholarship Integrating Faith and Accounting

A review of the literature integrating Christianity and accounting reveals that very little scholarly work has been done in this area. In addition, much of the work that does exist accepts, unquestioningly, much of the current composition of accounting practices and instead focuses on assisting religious organizations with compliance issues related to accounting standards. For example, an article by Cvach, Field, and Faris (1996) examines the treatment of church retirement plans by the Employee Retirement Income Security Act of 1974. Stock (1995) reviews fund accounting for nonprofits and provides illustrations of financial presentations for churches. Edwards (1990) discusses the importance of following proper accounting procedures to religious organizations and having an annual independent audit of their financial statements.

In these articles, basic foundational issues, such as why certain activities are reflected in the financial statements while others are excluded, are left untouched. This reticence appears to have two sources. First, Christian accountants, as members of the accounting profession, find it difficult to question basic tenets of the profession from which they draw their professional authority. Second, a tendency exists in the Christian community, as well as the broader society, to regard accounting practices as rigid and immune to interpretation. For example, Hooks (1992) examines the results of an AICPA survey that measured attitudes toward public accountants and found that 56% of the survey respondents thought that information presented in financial statement was precise. Chewning (1990) in his introduction to the chapter "A Theological Perspective on Accounting" in <u>Biblical Principles and Business: The Practice</u>, identifies this bias that many Christians bring to the discussion of Christianity and accounting by noting:

> I cannot help wondering how many of those who read it will have ever thought that biblical principles could be applied to accounting. . . . The chapter also shows how God's revealed moral principles are so encompassing as to include something that seems, on the surface at least, to be so removed from theology (p. 105).

Accounting as an Interpretive Art

The skepticism concerning the existence of a Christian perspective on accounting has resulted in a failure to examine critically foundational issues related to accounting. As a result of this failure, the assumption that accounting is a solely technical activity has remained largely unchallenged. Accounting is often portrayed "as a factual and objective form of knowledge untainted by social values or ideology; accounting data is apparently an asocial product almost untouched by human hand" (Loft, 1986, p. 137). Accounting is often represented as a set of neutral techniques that do no more than objectively record and reveal the results of organized activities. Accounting is treated as the mirror which reflects all the economic realities of the organization.

This assumption of neutrality is far too simplistic to be useful for the interpretation of accounting practices. In order to begin the discussion of integrating Christian faith and accounting, there must first be the acknowledgment that accounting is deeply embedded in a social context. Although accounting cannot claim to be solely social, attempting to understand it as a purely technical activity is impossible. Recently, more research has been conducted that views accounting as a profession that functions in a social environment. For example, Hooks (1992) examines how the accounting profession's response to public concerns can be explained as enhancements to the profession's self-interest. Roberts (1996) notes that all aspects of accounting that at first glance might seem to be relegated to the technical (for example, the measurements, techniques, and criteria of accounting) are in fact deeply influenced by social factors:

Accounting can be seen as a particular structure of meanings in terms of which the significance of organizational events is negotiated and defined, as the basis upon which expectations and demands upon staff are communicated and legitimized, and as the vehicle for the enactment and re-enactment of particular relations of power. The shift in attention from accounting to accountability is thus a shift from a preoccupation with technique and its refinement, to social practices and consequences (p. 41).

Stewart (1995) is a powerful example of the insight into accounting that can be gained when accounting practices are critically examined. Stewart recognizes accounting as an interpretive art and suggests that the accountant does not provide information that should be uncontested; the accountant does not reveal a pre-existing reality:

> Accounts are not objectivistic in the sense of a pointer-reading science. To argue that accounting is like a barometer, or speedometer, for example, is to grossly misunderstand its nature. It is the softness, then, of accounting numbers that is the reason why managers are so interested in them for they can manipulate them where they may be motivated to do so (p. 637).

In contrast to the traditional view of accounting as an impassive recorder of fact, Stewart (1995) asserts that "Accounting is more like a photograph -- it is taken from a particular vantage point, with a particular lens, at a particular time, for a particular purpose. . . . Accounting is also constitutive, and people act on the basis of the picture which is painted" (p. 636). By placing accounting practice in a social context, Stewart is able to argue that social responsibility and concern for the common good must be integrated into the work of accountants, just as these qualities are assumed to be central to the work of other established professions. He asserts that it is critically important to see the act of giving an account as serving "larger human and environmental purposes and that the accountant is ultimately responsible to God whose gift of freedom makes us accountable" (p. 634). By relating the act of giving account to the biblical principle of accountability Stewart introduces a framework from which the Christian accountant can address the issue of integrating faith and accounting.

Shifting the Focus from Accounting to Accountability

Accountability pervades human relations and interactions. Willmott (1996) suggests that accountability practices are the ways through which people render the world, including themselves, both observable and reportable in those ways that are logical to other members in society. The main process through which organizations make themselves observable and reportable to society is through their financial accounting reports. Roberts (1991) suggests that "The power of accounting information in organizations arises from the way it has been institutionalized as the most important, authoritative and telling means whereby activity is made visible" (p. 359). Munro (1996) suggests that we see through accounts: "Accountability is about making the invisible visible" (p. 5).

Currently, accounting systems do not capture information on all organizational activities, as the earlier discussion on human resource accounting illustrated. Therefore, accounting systems provide limited visibility to particular issues, which results in the creation of the significant within organizations (Richardson, 1987). Burchell, Clubb, Hopwood, Hughes, and Nahapiet (1980) suggest that accounting, "no longer seen as a mere assembly of calculative routines, now functions as a cohesive and influential mechanism for economic and social management" (p. 6). This results in a situation where the activities that are accounted for communicate to users of financial information (both within and outside organizations), what they should consider to be important. Activities excluded from financial communications will typically find it more difficult to articulate their contributions to the profitability of their organizations. The restricted ability of these activities to be accountable for their actions can result in the diminished ability of these activities to compete for the limited resources of their organizations. Thus the current accounting framework creates a particular perception of organizational reality that eventually becomes a self-fulfilling prophesy. The Financial Accounting Standards Board (1996), in its first statement of accounting concepts, states, "Financial reporting should provide information that is useful to present and potential investors and creditors and others in making rational investment, credit, and similar decisions" (p.1014). Indeed, by excluding certain activities from participating in the financial reports, the accounting process eventually causes these unaccountable activities to wither to the point of being meaningless to the decision-making process.

Accountability also pervades our relationship with God; scripture contains numerous references to the principle of accountability. Harrison, Jr. (1990) notes, "Ultimately, all persons and all organizations are accountable to God because He owns all things (see Gen. 1:1; John 1:1-3)" (p. 111). Accountability is also related to God's system of order and authority: "God sits at the apex of the authority chain and grants . . . the authority that employers hold over employees (see Eph. 6:5)" (p. 112). With the principle of accountability supported by a broad base of information, it is possible for managers to make wise decisions and to be good stewards of God's creation. However, because of the limited financial information accounting systems provide in particular areas (human resources and environmental issues, for example), managers are not receiving the broad base of information needed to generate the wisest decisions possible. Therefore, since we are held accountable by God to be good stewards of his creation, we need to develop accounting systems that give an observable and reportable form to a much broader spectrum of business activities than currently exists. It is possible this will require developing accounting procedures that transcend the purely transactional approach that we now see dominating accounting practice.

Significance of Power Theory to Understanding Accounting Practices

The Christian accountant must be able to critically question the very foundation upon which the profession is built. This is often very difficult for the Christian accountant, since the professional socialization process is usually quite strong in accounting. A first step in achieving movement toward a Christian perspective on accounting is to shift away from a functionalist perspective and toward a power perspective on accounting. Power theory can be used by Christian accountants to facilitate a critical examination of their profession because it encourages professionals to question well-established practices of their profession.

The functionalist approach to professionalism identifies attributes that are believed to be necessary elements in meeting the needs of society or specific professional-client relationships (e.g., Barber, 1963; Littleton & Zimmerman, 1962; Parsons, 1954). A functionalist viewpoint offers a rather kind picture of the professions; professions are expected to prosper in accordance with their ability to help society, not because of their self-interest and desire for profit. In the following statement Burchell et al. (1980) summarize the functionalist perspective on accounting:

Accounting is seen to have an essence, a core of functional claims and pretensions. It is, or so we are led to believe, essentially concerned with the provision of "relevant information for decision making", with the achievement of a "rational allocation of resources" and with the maintenance of institutional "accountability" and "stewardship." Such functional attributes are seen as being fundamental to the accounting endeavor. Justifying the existence of the craft, they provide rationales for continued accounting action. (pp. 9-10)

The functionalist perspective views the justification for the authority of accounting in society to rest on the accounting profession's ability to provide society with information critical to the rational allocation of resources. The functionalist perspective excludes from consideration the possibility that accounting is attracted to activities that it believes are capable of maintaining and/or expanding accounting's place in society.

By the early 1970s, several researchers began to reject the functional assumptions that had tempered research on professionalism to that point in time and instead began to explore more attitudinal explanations for the development of professions (e.g., Freidson, 1970; Johnson, 1972; Larson, 1977). These theorists were the first to propose that the professionalization process involves elements of power and autonomy, not simply trust and service to society. Power theorists do not interpret common characteristics of professions, such as certification requirements and enforcement of a code of ethics, as evidence of the service ideal held by professions. Rather, these qualities represent tools used by professions to limit competition for their job territories and to cultivate the public trust needed to create and/or maintain legislative support and protection.

If professions are motivated to some degree by a desire to maintain and/or expand their positions of authority within society, it is then imprudent to accept professional practices without adequate evaluation. Christian accountants must not be swayed by the often considerable and compelling weight of professional pronouncements if they feel the pronouncements are motivated more by the profession's own self interest rather than concern for the public's well-being. For example, Hooks (1992) analyzes the appearance, substance and effect of the accounting profession's response to public criticism in the late 1980s. Hooks notes that some of the responses seemed to be more concerned with appearances and the profession's self interest rather than any substantive change. Hooks states:

Appearance of Concern for Public Interest: [Statements on Auditing Standards] SASs 56 and 57 codified current practice. . . . Therefore, they have probably had little impact, even on firms with internal standards that do not exceed the profession's requirements. SASs 60 and 61 are directives for increased internal communications. They do not call for more external communication, nor do they constitute "whistle blowing". These four standards provide an appearance of concern for the public interest in striving for more effective auditing. In doing so, they cause little change to the auditing business, and therefore increase public confidence at very little professional effort. (p.127)

Analyzing accounting from a power perspective it is clear that the main source of accounting's power in society is its ability to affect the very way in which we "see" organizational activities. Accounting "is coming to be recognised as not being independent of the very organisational and social contexts in which it operates. It is implicated in the specification of organisational boundaries and in the creation of a means of visibility which can penetrate into internal functioning of the contexts in which it operates. Perceived in such terms, accounting is a creative rather than merely reflective endeavour" (Hopwood, 1989, p. 141). By capturing only selected activities in its analyses, accounting "plays a role in constructing an organisational or social domain not only by its positive acts of creation and enablement but also by its equally significant acts of demarcation and exclusion" (p. 141). The activities traditionally included within accounting's field of vision serve to reinforce the functional image of accounting as a neutral facilitator of effective decision-making, ultimately strengthening the power position of accounting in society. This can be illustrated by examining a key event in the history of accounting which occurred in the early 1900s: the development of theories of standard costing and budgeting.

Development of Managerial Accounting

The development of standard cost models and budgeting has traditionally been regarded as an important stage in the development and refinement of accounting concepts and techniques, with no ulterior motive attached to it. Standard costing and budgeting are viewed as useful techniques employed by organizations to enhance their ability to manage existing operations and to make plans for future activities. In contrast to this functional perspective, Miller and O'Leary (1987) view standard costing as a calculative practice that is one component of a "wider modern apparatus of power which emerges conspicuously in the early years of this century. The concern of this form of power is seen to be the construction of the individual person as a more manageable and efficient entity" (p. 235).

Development of Standard Costing Procedures

Prior to the development of standard costing, accounting functioned solely as a reporter of historical fact, not as a strategic partner in assessing current operations and planning for the future. Standard costing provided management with a powerful new tool to quantify variances of actual from standard at several different levels of analysis: the total organization, the quantity and price of material or labor used in production, and even the time and wages of individuals within the organization. Miller and O'Leary (1987) note that standard costing and budgeting enabled managers to:

Render visible the inefficiencies of the individual person within the enterprise. In routinely raising questions of waste and inefficiency in the employment of human, financial and material resources, they supplemented the traditional concerns of accounting with the fidelity or honesty of the person. Cost accounting could now embrace also the individual person and make them accountable by reference to prescribed standards of performance. With this step accounting significantly extended its domain, enmeshing the person within a web of calculative practices aimed not only at stewardship but efficiency also. (p. 241)

Studying the development of the accounting profession from a power rather than a functional perspective encourages the Christian accountant to examine different potential motivations for the current practices of the accounting profession. Interpreting the aforementioned advancement in accounting from a power perspective, it is clear that the accounting profession benefited greatly from the development of standard costing and budgeting models. These techniques enabled the accounting profession to befriend itself to the emerging movement called scientific management, as well as the engineering profession. It also enhanced the reputation of accountants as providers of objective financial information about organizational activities and assured a place for accountants in the strategic planning process of organizations. In summary, one of the outcomes of the development of these costing techniques in the early years of this century was the increase of accounting's significance to organizations, a significance that remains to this day.

Standard costing and budgeting techniques had a very powerful impact on the lives of individuals within organizations. Individual employees could now be held to very specific standards of performance and held accountable for variances from expected performance levels. It is less clear how these accounting techniques made organizations more accountable to society. A Christian perspective on accountability requires that accountability be reciprocal; organizations should be accountable to society in the same way that employees are expected to be accountable to their employers.

Examining this situation from a power perspective, two possible explanations emerge. First, the authority of accounting stems in large part from its capacity to present information as if it were objective fact. Activities that require creative measurement techniques continue to be largely ignored by the accounting profession. Second, accounting "lives" within organizations and therefore tends to engage in activities that make its hosts happy. These two points can be illustrated by an examination of an emerging area of accounting known as environmental accounting. The current lack of an accounting for the impact of organizational activities on environmental resources illustrates the reluctance of the accounting profession to pursue non-traditional forms of measurement, as well as its concern with the maintenance of good relationships with its host organizations.

Environmental Accounting

In Genesis 1 God created an environment for Adam and Eve to live in that perfectly supported all their physical needs:

God said, "See I have given you every plant yielding seed that is upon the face of all the earth, and every tree with seed in its fruit; you shall have them for food. And to every   beast of the earth, and to every bird of the air, and to everything that creeps on the earth, everything that has the breath of life, I have given every green plant for food." And it was so. God saw everything that he had made, and indeed, it was very good (Genesis 1:29-31). God further charged man with responsibility for the ongoing care of the earth (Genesis 8:17). Man is to exercise dominion over the earth in such a way that the natural environment is not threatened, but rather flourishes. Bouma-Prediger (1998) presents several arguments for why it is critical that we care for God's creation. His eighth argument states:

God commands that we care for creation; authentic faith demands that we obey God; therefore we should care for creation. For example, the oft neglected Genesis 2:15 states   that God created humankind to serve and protect the earth. We are called by God to be earth keepers; therefore we should strive to keep the earth -- to lovingly care for it – just as God promises to keep us. (p. 292)

It is clear that God commands us to be respectful of the earth, and that we will be held accountable for our stewardship of the earth. In Revelation 11:18 we are told: "Nations raged, but your wrath has come, and the time for judging the dead, for rewarding your servants, the prophets and saints and all who fear your name, both small and great, and for destroying those who destroy the earth."

Currently, accounting systems do not provide users of financial reports with the necessary information to hold organizations accountable for their treatment of environmental resources. In response to this situation some members of the academic accounting community support developing a system of environmental accounting. Sefcik, Soderstrom, and Stinson (1997) define environmental accounting as the "understanding, recognition and incorporation of the impact of environmental issues upon a firm's traditional accounting sub-systems"

(p. 129). Green accounting, as it is called, is a new concept that has attracted a good deal of attention from the accounting research community since it first appeared in the 1980s. The main objective of green accounting is to require organizations to reflect on their financial statements activities which cause natural resources to be compromised.

As one way of accomplishing this objective, Rubenstein (1992) suggests the creation of natural asset trust accounts and natural capital accounts for essential natural resources. The value of these accounts would be based on the greater of potential clean-up costs or the estimated discounted cash value of the future productive value of the asset. The capitalized value of the natural asset would remain constant until the organization engaged in activities that caused the future productive value of the resource to be depleted. These activities would cause an entry to be made into the accounting system that would increase the natural resource expense account and increase the liability due to natural trust account. "This would disclose pollution levels in excess of levels sustainable by an ecosystem. This accounting would reflect a new social contract between business and the stakeholders to whom they are accountable" (p. 501). (See Appendix A for an example.)

Currently, organizations are not supportive of attempts to develop environmentally aware accounting systems. It is likely that organizations do not believe it is in their best interests to expand the scope of activities over which they can be held accountable. Also, organizations rarely support any new accounting technique that potentially increases the level of liabilities they are responsible for reporting. From the accounting profession's perspective, determining both the potential clean-up costs and the future productive value of assets involve estimation techniques that run counter to the profession's preference for certainty. Hence, although there appear to be accounting techniques that could be employed to communicate to stakeholders the impact of organizations' activities on the environment, the Financial Accounting Standards Board has yet to make any recommendations in this area. It appears that the accounting profession's current position on environmental accounting is inconsistent with God's intention to hold man accountable for responsible stewardship of his creation.

Conclusion

For the most part, the Christian community has left the accounting profession alone. This seems to be due largely to Christians accepting, unquestioningly, the functionalist view of the accounting profession. In order to develop a Christian perspective on accounting there must be willingness both to examine the foundational suppositions of the profession and to question if these suppositions are in accordance with biblical principles. Power theory can be used to encourage the type of critical analysis of the accounting profession that is necessary. Analyzing the accounting profession from a power perspective it is clear that current accounting practices have at times been motivated by the profession's self-interest as opposed to a desire to serve God's kingdom. It is the responsibility of Christian accountants both to encourage the profession to see more broadly its societal responsibilities and to encourage it to be guided by the biblical principle of accountability.

Do you agree?

References

Barber, B. (1963). Some Problems in the Sociology of the Professions. Daedalus, 669-688.

Bouma-Prediger, S. (1998). Why Care for Creation?: From Prudence to Piety. Christian Scholar's Review, 27, 277-297.

Boudreau, J. W. (1983). Economic Considerations in Estimating the Utility of Human Resource Productivity Improvement Programs. Personnel Psychology, 36, 551-576.

Boudreau, J. W. (1984). Decision Theory Contributions to Human Resource Management Research and Practice. Industrial Relations, 23, 198-217.

Boudreau, J. W., & Berger, C. J. (1985). Decision-theoretic Utility Analysis Applied to Employee Separations and Acquisitions. Journal of Applied Psychology, 70, 581-612.

Burchell, S., Clubb, C., Hopwood, A., Hughes, J., & Nahapiet, J. (1980). The Roles of Accounting in Organizations and Society. Accounting, Organizations and Society, 5, 5-27.

Byrnes, N., Melcher, R. A., & Sparks, D. (1998, October 5). Earnings Hocus-Pocus. Business Week, 134-142.

Carnevale, A. P., & Schulz, E. R. (1990, Supplement to July). Return on Investment: Accounting for Training. Training & Development Journal, (Suppl.), S1-S32.

Chewning, R. C. (1990). A Theological Perspective on Accounting. In R. C. Chewning (Ed.), Christians in the Marketplace Series Biblical Principles and Business: The Practice (pp. 105-106). Colorado Springs: Navpress.

Chua, W. F. (1986). Radical Developments in Accounting Thought. Accounting Review, 61, 601-632.

Cvach, G. Q., Field, K. M., & Faris, C. (1996). Distinguishing Church Plans Under ERISA and the Code. <u>The Tax Advisor, 27,</u> 338-340.

Edwards, R. K. (1990). Financial Accountability in Religious Organizations. <u>National Public Accountant, 35,</u> 16.

Financial Accounting Standards Board. (1996). <u>Original Pronouncements Accounting Standards</u> (Vol. 2). New York: Wiley & Sons.

Freidson, E. (1970). <u>Professional Dominance: The Social Structure of Medical Care.</u> New York: Atherton Press.

Harrison, W. T., Jr. (1990). Biblical Principles Applied to Accounting. In R. C. Chewning (Ed.), <u>Christians in the Marketplace Series Biblical Principles and Business: The Practice</u> (pp. 107-120). Colorado Springs: Navpress.

<u>Holy Bible, New Revised Standard Version.</u> Grand Rapids: Zondervan Corporation, 1990.

Hooks, K. L. (1992). Professionalism and Self Interest: A Critical View of the Expectations Gap. <u>Critical Perspectives on Accounting, 3,</u> 109-136.

Hopwood, A. (1989). Accounting and the Pursuit of Social Interests. In W. F. Chua, T. Lowe, & T. Puxty (Eds.), <u>Critical Perspectives in Management Control</u> (pp. 141-157). London: MacMillan.

Johnson, T. (1972). <u>Professions and Power.</u> London: MacMillan.

Jones, T. C. (1995). <u>Accounting and the Enterprise a Social Analysis.</u> London: Routledge.

Larson, M. (1977). The Rise of Professionalism. Berkeley: University of California Press.

Littleton, A., & Zimmerman, V. (1962). Accounting Theory: Continuity and Change. Englewood Cliffs, NJ: Prentice-Hall.

Loft, A. (1986). Towards a Critical Understanding of Accounting: The Case of Cost Accounting in the UK, 1914-1925. Accounting, Organizations and Society, 11, 137-170.

Miller, P., & O'Leary, T. (1987). Accounting and the Construction of the Governable Person. Accounting, Organizations and Society, 12, 235-265.

Munro, R. (1996). Alignment and Identity Work: The Study of Accounts and Accountability. In R. Munro, & J. Mouritsen (Eds.), Accountability: Power, Ethos & the Technologies of Managing (pp. 1-19). London: International Thomson Press.

Page, D. (1996). Three Basics For Leadership Development in Christian Colleges and Universities. The Journal of Biblical Integration in Business, 1996, 61-91.

Parsons, T. (1954). The Professions and Social Structure. In T. Parsons (Ed.), Essays in Sociological Theory (pp. 34-49). Glencoe, Illinois: Free Press.

Richardson, A. J. (1987). Accounting as a Legitimating Institution. Accounting, Organizations and Society, 12, 341-355.

Roberts, J. (1991). The Possibilities of Accountability. Accounting, Organizations and Society, 16, 355-368.

Roberts, J. (1996). From Discipline to Dialogue: Individualizing and Socializing Forms of Accountability. In R. Munro, & J. Mouritsen (Eds.), Accountability: Power, Ethos & the

Technologies of Managing (pp. 40-61). London: International Thomson Press.

Roslender, R. (1992). Sociological Perspectives on Modern Accountancy. London: Routledge.

Rubenstein, D. B. (1992). Bridging the Gap Between Green Accounting and Black Ink. Accounting, Organizations and Society, 17, 501-508.

Sefcik, S. E., Soderstrom, N. S., Stinson, C. H. (1997). Accounting Through Green-Colored Glasses: Teaching Environmental Accounting. Issues in Accounting Education, 12, 129-140.

Stewart, I. C. (1995). Accounting and Accountability: Double Entry, Double Nature, Double Identity. In M. L. Stackhouse, D. P. McCann, & S. J. Roels (Eds.), On Moral Business (pp. 635-641). Grand Rapids: Eerdmans.

Stock, S. W. (1995). Church Reporting Made Easy. Management Accounting, 76, 56-59.

Thomas, J. (1998). The Future - It Is Us. Journal of Accountancy, 186 (6), 23-24.

Von Brachel, J. (1997). Creating a Future. Journal of Accountancy, 184 (5), 69-71.

Willmott, H. (1996). Thinking Accountability: Accounting for the Disciplined Production of Self. In R. Munro, & J. Mouritsen (Eds.), Accountability: Power, Ethos & the Technologies of Managing (pp. 23-39). London: International Thomson Press.

Appendix A
Greening the Financial Statements[1]

Creation of a Natural Asset Trust Account Worth $50,000,000:
Assets:

Natural Asset Account	$50,000,000 Dr.	

Equity:

Natural Capital Account		$50,000,000 Cr.

Company engages in activities that deplete the productive value of natural resources by $10,000,000:
Entry in the company operating accounts:

Natural Resource Exp.	$10,000,000 Dr.	
Due to Natural Asset Account		$10,000,000 Cr.

Entry in the National Assets Trust Fund:

Due from Company	$10,000,000 Dr.	
Accumulated Depletion of National Assets Account		$10,000,000 Cr.

[1]Note: From "Bridging The Gap Between Green Accounting And Black Ink," by D. B. Rubenstein, 1992, <u>Accounting, Organizations and Society, 17,</u> p. 507.

Devotions in Accounting

By
Dr. Jack E. Bower
Eastern University

Integration as a Goal

A major goal of your Christian professors is to promote spiritual formation within students. Spiritual training is one of the unique functions we offer as Christian faculty. Students tend to compartmentalize their thinking into a spiritual realm and a business realm and often have great difficulty integrating the two. In your business classes, we will use the Bible as a casebook of God's interaction with those who choose to follow Him. Through probing Bible stories from a business perspective, you will learn to integrate business and faith and so will develop your ability to think inclusively.

Integration Defined

Our task as Christian business faculty is to provide tools to help you see the entire world through a spiritual perspective. When we are successful, you will apply spiritual principles to the business world and, conversely, will understand scripture with help from business principles. Then you will be able to think inductively by contrasting and comparing problem situations. You will be able to identify common elements between biblical principles and business situations presented inside or outside the classroom. When you are able to do this, true integration is taking place.

Pedagogy

Our attempts at integration will occur both systematically and spontaneously throughout the limited time we have with you. Professors always are looking for that "teachable moment." Friendships between professors and students will develop inside and outside the classroom and often will continue beyond graduation. The most intense times of mentoring will occur during office hours, but certainly the classroom provides the most consistent time of interaction and of probing biblical principles. It is absolutely essential that you view the classroom as a safe environment in which to express opinions different from those of the professor. Sometimes it is more critical for the professor to understand what you are saying than to express an opinion or insight. Your professors pray regularly for the gift of being able to gently challenge your reasoning without threatening your feelings of safety in expression. Spiritual formation is impossible without the Holy Spirit working in both the teacher and the student.

The following devotions integrate principles of accounting with principles from God's Word. After setting the stage with a series of core theological values, the devotions follow the topical outline of a typical accounting book.

Ten Core Theological Questions and Values

1. <u>Is your attitude about money a theological issue? Does it matter in terms of finding salvation?</u> The answer is yes! *Read Matthew 19:16-26; Mark 10:17-27; or Luke 18:18-27.* This is commonly referred to as the story of the "Rich Young Man" who "went away sad, because he had great wealth" (New International Version). The point of the story: Wealth is a hindrance to following Jesus. Poverty will not necessarily save a person, and wealth will not necessarily condemn a person to hell. It is simply more difficult for the rich to follow Jesus than for the poor.

2. <u>Can riches choke the Word of God so that it produces nothing?</u> Jesus loved to tell stories with heavenly meanings (parables). *Read Matthew 13:3-8, 18-23; Mark 4:3-8, 14-20; or Luke 8:5-8, 11-15.* Known as the "Parable of the Sower," the story teaches that God's Word is like seed sowed in the world. The seed sowed in thorns is liked the person who hears the Word but is choked by the lure of riches and the worries of this world. Concern for one's wealth keeps the seed from growing and limits the person's ability to respond to the Good News. This truth is corroborated by the fact that the Gospel is often more readily received and accepted in less financially affluent communities.

3. <u>Who do you trust for security?</u> From God's perspective, the answer

to this question involves the concept of idolatry. (To "idolize" means to feel excessive devotion for something or someone.) *Read Matthew 6:19-24.* Jesus said your heart will follow your treasure. The world teaches us to trust in our wealth for security. Wall Street and Hollywood have become holy ground for the idolatry of wealth and power. Should you save for your retirement? Yes, because our culture does not place the burden of elder care upon the children. But the real issue is who—or what—you really trust to take care of you: your pension plan or God.

4. <u>Is greed good?</u> One of the finance Web sites runs a column called "Greed Is Good." Greed means never having enough—never enough cars, homes, share of corporate ownership, bonds, and so on. It is never enough. *Read Luke 12:13-21.* God did not call the man who hoarded his possessions wicked, but a fool. Jesus said the greedy are foolish. They are mistaken about life. Abundant life, according to God, does not arise from or necessitate an abundance of possessions.

5. <u>How important are generosity and repaying wrongs?</u> In many cultures a tax collector or tax-forms preparer negotiates the tax owed with an individual taxpayer and then negotiates for a lesser amount from the taxing authority. The difference belongs to the tax preparer as fees earned. Rome used such a system in the time of Jesus, and the Italian government today uses a similar system. A senior tax collector, Zacchaeus, operating under such a system is featured in one Bible story. *Read Luke 19:1-10.* Zacchaeus' response to Jesus' message was one of extreme generosity. He gave half of his possessions to the poor and repaid those whom he had cheated an amount worth four times what he'd taken from them! In the words of Jesus, "Today salvation has come to this house" (NIV). Certainly poverty does not mean moral purity, and wealth does not bar salvation. But in this story, Zacchaeus traded his wealth for salvation. He was a much different tax collector after his encounter with Jesus.

6. <u>How important is equal treatment of the wealthy and the poor?</u> *Read James 2:1-9.* James condemned those who made class distinctions in the church. Who are the leaders of the church today? Do we elect or

appoint into leadership positions the poor or the rich? We tend to equate success in the business world and success in the spiritual world, but basing decisions about leadership positions on a person's wealth are wrong. According to James, "God has chosen those who are poor in the eyes of the world to be rich in faith" (NIV).

7. How critical is economic justice to salvation? *Read James 5:1-6.* James harshly condemned the wealthy for not paying a fair wage, and he also condemned an unjust distribution system. This passage also establishes the "Rust Principle": If you have possessions that are idle and rusting away such as an old car or boat or motorcycle, you have too many possessions. Ownership carries responsibility. You need to get rid of assets you do not use. Jesus said, "Go, sell your possessions and give to the poor" (Matthew 19:21, NIV).

8. In the New Testament, what was the goal of giving to the church? Sharing resources was a central characteristic of the early church. *Read Acts 2:44-47.* What are our goals today in giving to the church? Examine your church budget and see how much is allocated toward serving the poor. For example, what is your church doing to meet the needs of the homeless?

9. Does wealth conflict with the spiritual nature of the Kingdom? The Old Testament details God's *physical* blessings upon those who follow Him, and the Kingdom had a physical presence in the nation of Israel and in God's Holy Temple. Did Jesus make a fundamental paradigm shift in the Kingdom of God from the physical to the spiritual? *Read John 18:36-37.* The *spiritual* Kingdom promised by Jesus does not promise physical wealth as a sign of God's blessings, nor is wealth considered evil (for example, the streets of heaven are described as being of pure gold). There is also no command to repudiate the wealth of the physical world. We are to live in the world but not become seduced by it (James 4:4; Luke 9:25).

10. It is impossible to provide for the physical needs of others unless you possess some resources of your own? Do you ever feel a sense of inconsistency in the passages that deal with wealth? *Read Hebrews*

13:2 and Matthew 6:19. We are commanded to be hospitable, but hospitality takes resources. It is easer for the person with an extra bed to entertain the stranger? How much to own and how much to give away is a constant dilemma for North American Christians. The critical issue, according to Paul in 1 Timothy 6:17, is *hope.* Do we place our "hope in God" or our "hope in wealth, which is so uncertain" (NIV)?

Double-Entry Accounting

What is the origin of double-entry accounting? Was modern accounting divinely inspired? Two professions, accounting and law, maintain justice and social order. Our God is a God of justice. *Read James 5:4-5.* How do you know what you owe the laborers without an accounting system? How do you know what is a just profit unless you record revenue and all expenses (the matching principle)? As trading partnerships developed in the 1200s, the church had a great concern over the calculation of a just profit. The timing was perfect; the great theologian St. Thomas Aquinas had both the opportunity and the motive to develop the accounting system we have today.[1]

Debits and Credits

The most famous credit in the Bible was the faith of Abraham (Genesis 15:6). *Read Romans 4:1-8.* Paul quotes the reference to Abraham's credit seven times in the New Testament. The business term "credit" actually came from the Greek translation of the Bible known as the Septuagint. Paul was raised as a Greek and would have studied the Septuagint. In God's accounting equation, we are an accounts receivable while credits decrease our debit balance. The term credit also is used in Romans 4:4 when referring to the increase in wages payable. Can our human credits save us? Said another way, can we earn our salvation? The answer is no. Only the blood of Jesus Christ frees us from sin and death.

Measurement Issues

What does accounting measure? Not all financial transactions are measured by the accounting system. Signing contracts or determining prices significantly impacts the organization's finances, but these actions are not recorded in the accounting system. An organization's most important asset usually is its human capital, which also is not recorded in the accounting system. <u>What does God's spiritual accounting system measure?</u> Actions, yes, but also motives. *Read Matthew 5:27-29, 43-48.* We are called to have pure thoughts and pure hearts with unbounded love for our enemies. God sees our actions, knows our hearts, and judges our motives.

The Entity Concept
The concept of "Separate Entity" is critical to the ability of the accounting equation to properly record transactions and measure performance. <u>What type of entity is God? What type of entity is our spiritual life?</u> *Read John 10:24-38.* The "God Head" acts like a partnership. The relationship between the Father, Son, and Holy Spirit is one of mutual agency. We, on the other hand, are more like a publicly held corporation that requires outside investments to grow spiritually. We receive investments from parents, friends, and from the Holy Spirit at work within our lives.

The Accounting Equation
<u>If God needed to keep accounting records and used the accounting equation, what would the equation look like?</u> The assets would include all of heaven and earth. Inventory would have included mankind before the fall. After the fall, we became accounts receivable to God. Each of our sins increases our accounts receivable on God's books as well as an increase to His liability account called sin. A God of justice must punish sin. *Read Matthew 6:9-13 and Genesis 15:6.* The scriptures consistently equate sin with debt and equate faith as a credit against our accounts receivable held by God.[2]

Generally Accepted Accounting Principles (GAAP)
<u>How critical is trust in human relationships?</u> In financial relationships between investors and corporations, trust is defined as Generally Accepted Accounting Principles (GAAP). Our relationship with God is also one of trustworthiness. *Read Luke 16:10-13.* Jesus calls us to be trustworthy in our handling of worldly wealth so that God can trust us with true spiritual riches.[3]

Revenue Recognition

<u>When is revenue recognized?</u> This question continually presents itself on the pages of the *Wall Street Journal* in a section called "Money and Investing." Corporations, analysts, and shareholders argue principles of revenue and expense recognition with the Securities and Exchange Commission (SEC)—and sometimes in the courts. Humans do the same thing with God. We suppress our conscience and rationalize away sin until we convince ourselves that God does not see or care about our little injustices or careless words. *Read Matthew 12:33-37*. Jesus says everything we say is recorded and that we will face our sins on the Day of Judgment.

Money Measurement

Accounting uses money as a unit of measure. <u>If it cannot be expressed as money, is it recorded as a journal entry?</u> The Old Testament gave the Jewish nation some specific measures of sin. Jesus shifted the paradigm and changed the unit of measure. *Read Matthew 5:13-16.* Our call as Christians is to be salt and light in a fallen world by changing the unit of measure. We ask others to consider following Jesus, making Him Lord of their lives, and then we ask them to see every transaction through a new spiritual lens.

Journal Entries

High school and college students often are required to keep a written journal of their experiences as a method of learning through writing. Jesus commonly used stories to instruct, and the scriptures are a sort of journal of the Jewish nation, the life of Jesus Christ, and the history of the church. Luke, for example, provides the most orderly account of Jesus' life. In journalizing for a business, materiality is always an issue; only the material or significant events are recorded, requiring a great deal of judgment on the part of the accountant. The same issue of materiality faced the Gospel writers as they journalized the life of Jesus. *Read John 21:24-25.* In our spiritual lives, Jesus calls us to be accountable for the material issues of life. Every sin hurts God, but we tend to minimize our own sins and magnify the sins of others. Jesus said, "Why do you look at the speck of sawdust in your brother's eye and pay no attention to the plank in your own eye?" (Matthew 7:3,

NIV). (This is a little Godly humor regarding our decisions to spiritually journalize what is material and what is not material.)

The Matching Principle

Periodicity and the matching principle attempt to provide for a trustworthy net income. Adjustments to the accounting records recognize revenue and expenses in the proper time period. It is an essential accounting principle for trustworthy earnings, but it does not work in terms of salvation. As humans, we have a tendency to match our good deeds against our bad deeds and then feel good about ourselves. <u>Can a dedicated life of service to God guarantee salvation?</u> The answer is no! Only through the blood of Jesus Christ can we find salvation. It is not earned, and it is certainly not a matter of doing more good deeds than bad deeds. *Read Ephesians 2:4-9.* Salvation is a gift from God, pure and simple.

Closing Entries

Closing entries move or transfer the balances from the temporary accounts into the permanent accounts. For nonbelievers, their spiritual books will close when they face death and transition from the physical world to the spiritual world. All temporary accounts on this earth will be closed. *Read 1 John 3:11-20.* When we accept Jesus Christ as King of our lives, the books of our old lives are closed and we pass from death to life. The names of those who choose life are recorded in the "book of life." The Apostle John says in verse 17 that the evidence of this transfer from death to life is the way we address the needs of the poor with our material wealth.

Trial Balance

We are encouraged to evaluate our lives continually in light of the Word of God. This can happen in times of prayer, and it happens for many Christians during Communion. *Read 1 Corinthians 11:23-34.* The accounting records also are periodically examined to see if they are in balance. The test of the system's balance is called a trial balance. Until a proper trial balance is made, the accountant can be in error and not know it. So it is with our spiritual lives. Periodically, we need to stop and gain perspective, evaluate our lives, and determine if we are in balance with the will of God for our lives.

Merchandising Operations 1: Inventory

<u>What does our spiritual inventory look like?</u> Jesus describes us as being fruit-bearing trees and branches. *Read Matthew 7:15-20.* If our heart, soul, strength, and mind are committed to God, we will produce good fruit. If we are rotten on the inside, we will produce bad fruit. Jesus said, "Thus, by their fruit you will recognize them" (NIV). What kind of fruit are you bearing for the Kingdom of God?

Merchandising Operations 2

Read Luke 19:11-27. The concept of trading, buying low, and selling high is described in this passage, commonly known as the "Parable of the Talents." This passage might illustrate the investment of spiritual gifts. Most often in scripture, however, our spiritual inventory is not described as something we purchase and then sell. Instead, it is more like the inventory of the farmer, through which seeds grow into a harvest if they are properly planted and watered. *Read John 15:1-2 and 2 Corinthians 9:6-11.* Sometimes we plant, and sometimes we water. Our challenge is to sow generously in order to reap generously.

Merchandising Operations 3

<u>Does God use a periodic or perpetual inventory system?</u> In God's accounting system, humans became accounts receivable after the fall. The inventory of the earth is under His constant care. *Read Matthew 10:29-31.* Consider the number of people on the earth and the number of hairs on each head. Can God do exponential math or what? Jesus indicated that God uses a perpetual inventory system.

Full Disclosure

Financial reporting requires full disclosure. This means that significant events and financial transactions that could influence a decision-maker must be explained in the financial statement or its footnotes. <u>But how are we to handle spiritual reporting to each other?</u> *Read Matthew 6:1-6.* In God's system of spiritual reporting, He knows all and sees all. But in reporting to each other, the system is just the opposite of full disclosure. We are, in fact, to keep our good deeds a secret from friends and, if married, even from our spouses. The left hand should not know the good deeds of the right hand.

Principles of Cost-Benefit, Control, Compatibility, and Flexibility

Accounting software supports operations and is essential to the continued growth of the company. Computer system design follows four principles: cost-benefit, control, compatibility, and flexibility. The same principles hold true for evaluating the church fellowship to which we belong. *Read Ephesians 5:10.* Questions about fellowship and where we belong in the Kingdom are some of the most difficult spiritual questions we face on this earth. Paul's admonition was to pray and search for God's will in our lives.

Subsidiary Ledgers

Accounting systems use subsidiary ledgers to group accounts receivable, accounts payable, inventory, and so on. <u>Does God use subsidiary ledgers?</u> *Read Revelation 20:11-12.* Yes, the book of life is a subsidiary ledger. Pray that your name is found in the book of life!

Bank Reconciliation

Bank reconciliations are a reality check. The bank statement generally is the transactional truth, and our accounting records are adjusted to conform to the economic reality of the bank. *Read 2 Corinthians 5:18-19.* Paul wrote, "God...gave us the ministry of reconciliation" (NIV). There is a spiritual reality that God will punish sin. There is also the reality that God has reconciled the world to Himself through Jesus Christ. The accountant has a duty to reconcile the company books to the economic reality of the bank's transactions. We, as Christians, have a ministry of reconciliation between the world and God the Father.

Internal Control

Internal control is absolutely critical for a business to function according to management's established procedures and policies. <u>What are God's internal controls in your life that keep you true to Him?</u> Internal control policies include but are not limited to the following:
Authorization—The Bible "judges the thoughts and attitudes of the heart" (NIV). *Read Hebrews 4:12-13.*

Recording transactions—The Holy Spirit helps us determine what is sin. *Read Acts 5:3.*

Documents and records—An all-knowing God does not need to keep records. Yet in our own lives of producing fruit, we are not to record or show our good deeds.

Limited access—Our conscience helps us to limit our exposure to sin and to know what is good and beneficial for spiritual growth.

Periodic independent verification—As brothers and sisters in Christ, we hold each other accountable for what is good and pure and holy.

Separation of duties—Each of us in the Kingdom has a calling, a duty to perform. We are not all feet or hands.

Sound personnel policies—Choose your friends wisely, for "a companion of fools suffers harm" (Proverbs 13:20, NIV).

The Credit Dilemma

Every business is concerned about the time it takes to collect accountants receivable. We call this ratio "days sales outstanding," or DSO. The critical factor affecting this ratio is the companies' credit policies. Trusting everyone with unlimited credit will guarantee business failure. *Read Matthew 5:38-42 and Proverbs 22:26-27.* On the one hand, Jesus calls upon us to be very generous in our policies of lending. You are to love your enemies and lend to the person who wants to borrow from you. You also are encouraged from the passage in Proverbs not to provide the collateral or inventory for debt. Setting credit policy is a very difficult area for Christians who want to trust everyone while securing the financial health of their businesses.

Short-Term Investments

Short-term investments fall into one of three categories: trading securities, available-for-sale securities, or held-to-maturity Securities. <u>What type of security are you, spiritually speaking?</u> We all would like to be in the "held-to-maturity" category. Staying faithful to God takes reliance upon Him and emotional strength and commitment. *Read Romans 7:14-25.* We all want to strive mightily against sin. Yet often we fail in the struggle, and we realize our own weaknesses at that point. Unfortunately, the struggle does not get easier with age. For most people, emotional strength decreases with age. For example, as we age, we cry at events that never would have affected us in our youth. Only by the power of God can we remain faithful for a lifetime.

Allowance for Doubtful Accounts

Every business is forced to face the fact that every customer is not going to pay his or her bill—some due to a lack of financial resources and others due to their swindling nature. To quote King David in Psalm 37:21, "The wicked borrow and do not repay" (NIV). Even believers, in dealing with each other, have a sinful nature. To quote Paul, "For all have sinned and fall short of the glory of God" (Romans 3:23, NIV). The correct accounting treatment is to create an allowance for doubtful accounts and estimate the amount of nonpayment. *Read 1 John 1:5-10.* The good news is that God will not fail us. He is trustworthy yesterday, today, and tomorrow. He is a consistent friend and source of power and light for doing good in our lives. We serve an awesome God!

Inventory 1

We are part of God's inventory. Can you name God's asset list from Genesis 1?
heavens, earth, and light
air ("sky")
land, seas, and vegetation
the sun, moon, and stars
water creatures and birds
land creatures and humans
God rested!

Read Genesis 2:15. God gave to mankind a charge to work the earth and care for it. After the fall of mankind, the ground was cursed; then entered painful toil, thorns, and thistles into the human experience (Genesis 3:17-18). Human beings confuse possession with ownership. God gave us possession of the earth, but it still belongs to Him. Humans are the caretakers, not the owners. In Leviticus 25:23 God said, "The land is mine and you are but aliens and my tenants" (NIV). This fact also speaks to the environmental debate. Regrettably, many people choose to ignore the environmental crisis, while others go to the opposite extreme and see created things as gods. "Mother Nature" has taken on a spirituality of her own, and defining her has become a religion.

Inventory 2

God created us as inventory; after the fall, we were reclassified as accounts receivable. <u>Do we still belong to God? Do our bodies belong to Him?</u> *Read 1 Corinthians 6:20.* What does it mean to honor God with your body? How you answer the question of ownership will determine your position on the abortion issue. If we own our bodies, then a mother has the right to terminate the life within her. If it is God's body, the mother's rights are limited to His rules and principles. Respect for life at conception is a sound biblical principle.

Inventory 3

<u>Does God use a LIFO or FIFO inventory system?</u> *Read Matthew 19:30; 20:1-16; Mark 10:31; or Luke 13:30*: "There are those who are last who will be first, and first who will be last" (NIV). God uses a LIFO system. What does this mean? We can infer from Matthew 20 that those who accept God early in the history of the Kingdom will be last in line, and those who accept God at the end of the period will be the first to enter heaven. Is this what these passages teach us?

Long-Term Assets 1

Jesus is not against investing in long-term assets. He is against investing in the wrong long-term assets. Repeatedly the scriptures encourage us to lay up treasure in heaven. *Read John 14:1-3.* Is the place Jesus is preparing for us a room in God's house or a mansion of our own? The translators of the King James Bible used the word "mansion" to represent the place prepared for the saints, and songs such as "Mansion just over the hilltop" made the idea popular.[4] <u>Do you expect to find great personal wealth in heaven?</u>

Long-Term Assets 2

Land tenure was everything in Old Testament times. Real wealth, or what was known as a true estate, was only real if it included land. Hence the term a "real estate." *Read Leviticus 25:23-28.* God was very concerned about property rights and the wealth it controlled. Is this how we define wealth today? No, today intangible assets compose most of our modern wealth. We use the expression "capitalization" to refer to modern wealth. "Equity capitalization" is the market price of the shares multiplied by the number of shares outstanding. Shares are intangible assets that define a legal right. The critical question is, "To what extent is this wealth the product of injustice?" We have a moral responsibility to analyze the profit-making activities and the social agendas of the corporations in which we invest.

Long-Term Assets 3
Often the ownership of assets is a disputed accounting issue. Leases, for example, can be operating leases or capital leases. Capital leases are recorded on the balance sheet, and operating leases are not. Scripture teaches that our bodies are not our own; the earth and everything in it belongs to God. What about your soul? Do you own your soul? Can you sell it to the devil? *Read John 13:21-30.* What protection do you have against Satan? Two of the most difficult chapters in the Bible, Romans 9 and 10, address the relationship between God, humans, and Satan. Actually, we should read Romans 9, 10, and 11 together for a full understanding of free will and predestination. We have the indwelling and protection of the Holy Spirit for our souls. God holds the title, and we have unlimited use of this asset. Our souls are an operating lease from God.

Deferred Gains and Losses
One of the most complex topics in the revelation of God is deferred redemption. The Old Testament atonement process is described in Leviticus 4 and 16. *Read Romans 3:21-31.* The New Testament writers tell us that sins before the death of Jesus Christ were unpunished; they were deferred until the time of Christ. This is a difficult concept. So is the concept of deferred gains and losses for like-kind exchanges. Deferred gains and suspended losses are reflected in adjustments to basis. Like Old Testament sins, they are suspended in time, waiting for redemption to occur.

Debt 1: God's Liability Account
The scriptures consistently equate sin with debt. We owe God for our trespasses, what we call "sin." Jesus came to "forgive us our debts, as

we also have forgiven our debtors" (Matthew 6:12, NIV). *Read Matthew 18:23-35.* It is very interesting to study cultural patterns of perception toward debt. In Jesus' time, debt could mean imprisonment. There are no debtors' prisons in the United States, but U.S. culture still debates the proper punishment for debt as defined in U.S. bankruptcy laws.

Debt 2: Ideal Capital Structure

Is debt good or bad? Excessive credit card debt has become a financial epidemic in some cultures. Nonprofit organizations offering debt counseling abound. What is the proper attitude for a Christian to have toward debt? *Read Romans 13:1-10.* Paul encouraged us not to be in debt to anyone for anything, except to carry a debt of love for each other. To be totally debt-free should be a personal financial goal. In the world of corporate finance, the most profitable debt level depends on the stability of earnings over time; hence, the debt rating or cost of debt. For a company, an ideal capital structure balancing both debt and equity can contribute significantly to earnings. The ideal capital structure for an individual or family in U.S. culture often means the assumption of a mortgage and home ownership. Over time, home ownership also can contribute significantly to savings.

Debt 3: Repayment Period

For how long a time period should we finance debt? The Old Testament law contained a redemption principle for debt every seven years, which included returning land to its original holders every fifty years. *Read Deuteronomy 15:1-6 and Leviticus 25:8-12.* Should we forgive debt every seven years? Jesus Christ fulfilled the Jubilee concept of debt forgiveness. Luke 4:18-19 records Jesus, at the beginning of His ministry, reading scripture in the synagogue in order to tell the audience that he was the personification of the year of Jubilee. Jesus came to earth as a man to free us from the chains of sin and death. As followers of Jesus Christ, we have the same mission. We become the reverse of mortgage brokers. We tell others how to be debt-free!

Partnerships

Partnerships were a common business entity in New Testament times.

John and James (the sons of Zebedee) and Simon Peter were in a partnership. *Read Luke 5:6-11.* Like Simon Peter, John, and James, we are called to join a partnership that fishes for lost souls. How do you feel about the term "partner" versus that of the term "brother or sister"? Paul used the term "partner" when referring to Christians with whom he had a working relationship—for example, Titus (2 Corinthians 8:23) and Philemon, the master of Onesimus (Philemon 17). Is this a good biblical term that we should use today?

Corporate Form

What is the meaning of the term "incarnation"? The word means, "to take human form." When God became man, Jesus was the incarnation. How human was Jesus? Could he miss the nail with a hammer and smash this finger? Did he ever trip and fall down? *Read Mark 11:12-14.* The word "incorporate" means, "to make into a body." A corporation is a creature created by state statute. It is a type of incarnation. It is the assumption of a body by a legal entity that is then owned and directed by the shareholders. What we look forward to is the reverse of incarnation, when the church is transformed into the bride of Christ.

Common Shareholders

We are shareholders in heaven. But are we common shareholders or preferred shareholders? Consider our rights as shareholders. We have no votes, and we are callable souls in God's eyes. This means we hold convertible preferred shares and are looking forward to being called and converted. Dividends can be considered gifts by the shareholders. Does God pay dividends? Peter said that we receive the gift of the Holy Spirit when we accept the Lord in baptism (Acts 2:38). The difference between corporate dividends and spiritual dividends is that the spiritual dividends are not proportionate to the number of shares we hold. *Read Ephesians 4:7-8.* Common translations for the way spiritual gifts are distributed are "apportioned" and "allocated."

Discontinued Operations

The income statement is divided into income from continuing operations and all other one-time events that happened during a particular year. Many companies also have discontinued operations, which usually are unprofitable activities that management wants to terminate. *Read Ephesians 4:22-24 and 1 Peter 1:14-16.* As Christians we are called "to put off your old self, which is being corrupted by its deceitful desires, to be made new in the attitude of your minds" (NIV). We are to discontinue the spiritually unproductive activities in our lives.

Statement of Shareholders Equity

Business organizations generally fall into three organizational forms: sole proprietorship, partnership, or corporation. What kind of business form do you have as a Christian? Are you a sole proprietorship who tries to stand on your own? Are you a partner with God? In partnerships, the parties share an equality, and we know we cannot assume equality with God. In stead, God is the principal investor and uses the Holy Spirit and other people to mold and shape us into His image. *Read Isaiah 64:8-9 or 45:9.* In accounting, the "Statement of Shareholders' Equity" discloses the different types of investors in a corporation? What would your "Statement of Shareholders' Spiritual Equity" look like? What are the supporting ligaments of your spiritual growth? You might have one column for parents, one for teachers, and another for brothers and sisters in Christ. For all of us, the statement would include this disclaimer: "God is still working on me."

Share Value

The word "value" is perhaps the most overused term in finance. We hear questions such as "Does it add value?" or "Is the stock overvalued?" The term "Christian values" might be the most overused term on family radio. During a time when values are in question, it is good to remind ourselves of the value God places on each one of us. *Read Matthew 10:31 or Luke 12:7.* Perhaps God's response to Jesus' baptism as recorded in Matthew 3:17 is the clearest answer we have to questions about our identity. God answered three questions for Jesus (NIV):

Who am I? "This is my Son."

What is our relationship? "Whom I love."

How am I doing? "With him I am well pleased."

Each believer needs to hear those same words from the Holy Spirit that dwells within him or her.

Statement of Cash Flows 1

A common expression in the corporate financial world is "Cash is King." Everyone knows that "cash concerns" rule. Employees will tolerate a lot of internal problems as long as their paychecks do not bounce. In the nonprofit sector, cash flow is even more important. *Read John 18:33-37.* The spiritual world has a King whose name is Jesus Christ. As Christians we are members of the Lord's Kingdom. <u>What difference has his kingship made in your life?</u>

Statement of Cash Flows 2

What would a standard distribution curve look like if all of Jesus' believers were placed on it according to their prayer life? The majority of Christians, centered around the mean, maintain a consistent prayer life. They find time to seriously study scripture, and they feed themselves with regular worship. They do not need continual spiritual investment by others. The left tail of the distribution curve most likely would be pastors who are so efficient in their spiritual operations that they can invest in the spiritual maintenance and support of others. The right side of the curve most like would be those individuals who need continual emotional and spiritual support to remain faithful to God. They have negative spiritual operations that need to be financed by others. *Read Ephesians 4:14-17.* The business world divides the activities of an entity into three categories: operations, investments, and financing. Some businesses support themselves from operations. Others, like pastors, are efficient at operations and can make investments in fixed assets. Still others, like most of the "dot-com" companies, have negative operations and need continual financing by outsiders in order to survive. <u>Are your daily spiritual operations self-sufficient? Do you get enough time alone with God and in the fellowship of the saints to empower yourself spiritually?</u>

Statement of Cash Flows 3

A positive cash flow from operations (CF Op.) is a measure of financial strength. Financial ratios, which use net income, also can be modified to assess the strength of cash flows by substituting CF Op. in place of net income. For example, the measure for margin is net income over sales. The ratio of CF Op. over sales produces a ratio similar to margin. What is a good measure of our spiritual strength? *Read Matthew 17:20-21.* Most Christians acknowledge that faith is the key to being strong for God. Imagine for a moment a tree in the morning sunshine after an ice storm the night before with all the branches covered in ice. The tree is blocking your view of the sun, but the branches covered in ice are refracting the sun's light. So it is with faith. Like the refractions of the sun's light, we only can see the evidence of faith. "Now faith is being sure of what we hope for and certain of what we do not see" (Hebrews 11:1). Pray that God gives you the faith to be strong!

Financial Statement Analysis 1

Anyone who has ever purchased a used car knows that the perception often is not the final reality. There are generally significant problems with a used car that are not perceived before the purchase is made. The same can be said for purchasing "used" shares. Shares purchased on an organized exchange are previously owned and are, therefore, used. With used cars and shares of stock, the front-end perception often is better than the final result or end perception. Minimizing the difference between perception and reality is the purpose of financial statement analysis. The attempt is to remove surprises by thoroughly studying the company's strategic analysis and available financial data. Likewise, we should carefully analyze new activities in our lives. Like the used car or that "perfect" stock pick, sin looks better on the front-end than on the back-end. The old adage "The grass looks greener on the other side" holds true when we choose what looks like the easy path over God's will for our lives. *Read Luke 15:11-32,* commonly knows as the "Parable of the Lost Son." The father in the story represents God the Father, and the good news is that He welcomes us back home after a reckless lifestyle. Sin always looks better on the front-end than on the back-end.

Financial Statement Analysis 2

There are five primary factors we use to evaluate shares of corporate stock: risk, technical analysis, value, liquidity, and profitability. (And there are six factors if you include prayer.) <u>What factors do we use to evaluate the investment of our time in godly activities?</u> *Read 2 Timothy 3:14-17.* Most faith groups use the Bible to rule out certain activities, and other groups use the Bible to rule in activities. All Christian faith groups, including the Roman Catholic Church, search the scriptures for commands, examples, and necessary inferences. Are we commanded in the scriptures to build houses for the poor, as do volunteers for Habitat for Humanity? No! However, it certainly is a necessary inference to "love your neighbor as yourself." Evaluating the use of our time and our money requires considerable wisdom from above. Praying before a share purchase or a commitment of volunteer time will help to create value.

Share Price

The formula for share price is Price = $D_1/(k-g)$. Why does the formula use D_1, the future dividend, instead of Do, the current dividend? Because the share-price formula is a derivative of the present value formula, $PV = FV/(1+k)n$. The stock market bases the share price on the future performance of the company, not on the present performance. So it is with the Christian life. Our definition of value is based upon a belief in future events, not present events. Elton Trueblood wrote a book titled *A Place to Stand.*[5] The resurrection of Jesus Christ is our place to stand. *Read John 11:25-26.* <u>Where is your place to stand?</u>

Change in Accounting Principles

Sometimes a business must acknowledge that an accounting practice they have been using is not in the best interest of fair disclosure. AOL, for example, booked its distribution of free trial disks as an asset instead of as an expense. Through pressure from the financial community, AOL took a one-time hit and corrected the financial statements. Share price increased as a result. *Read 1 John 1:8-10.* Salvation is all about coming clean. Acknowledging and confessing our sins is the beginning point for the cleansing that comes from the blood of Jesus Christ.

International Accounting Standards

What do we mean by the expression "The world is getting smaller"? What kinds of businesses are forced to think and act globally? Consider the percentage of foreign revenues for some major U.S. companies: Exxon, 77%; General Motors, 31%; Mobil, 67%; IBM, 61%.[6] Did Jesus have a global perspective? Yes! He instructed his disciples to take his message to the whole world (Matthew 28:19-20). Perhaps the clearest example of Jesus' global perspective is the so-called "Parable of the Good Samaritan," in which the hero is a foreigner. *Read Luke 10:25-37.* The "love-your-neighbor" principle is universal. We have a moral obligation to care about people we have never met who suffer from poverty and affliction. Lord, give us your eyes for the poor.

Business Consolidations and Minority Interest

Business consolidations should be an attempt to add value to each company. Occasionally they do succeed in raising the share prices of both companies. The resulting combination is a larger and hopefully more economically successful operation. The parent corporation can purchase the shares in a friendly "takeover" arranged between the two boards of directors or in a hostile manner often resulting in a bidding war between rivals. The shares not obtained by the parent are called the "minority interest." There are several parallels in the spiritual realm. *Read 1 Corinthians 6:19-20.* Jesus paid for our sins on the cross, and we become one with Him in a consolidated relationship. For some believers, it is a friendly merger nurtured by parents and Bible schoolteachers. For others, it seems to be an all-out fight between the forces of God and the forces of Satan. Successful contributions from God, parents, and children (the subsidiary entity) always increase value. Our consolidated statements then reflect God's ownership control in our lives, and the minority interest indicates the portions of our lives that we hold back, unwilling to give to God.

Equity Method

The equity method is unique to the financial landscape of the United States. It follows the notion that "we are they, and they are us." When the investment target has earnings, the investor has earnings. When the investment target pays dividends, the value of the investor's investment decreases. Consider the relationship between brothers and sisters in Christ. We follow a similar equity principle. *Read 1 Corinthians 12:12-20.* We cry with those who grieve and rejoice with those who are joyful. We treat each other as family. We are they, and they are us; we are one body. We influence each other, but we do not control each other; this is the equity method of spirituality.

Goodwill or God's Will

Providence is a biblical concept, and so is predestination. *Read Romans 8:28-30.* God has a plan for each of us, and we pray for a spirit of revelation to know and understand His will for our lives. Most Christians say that it is by His grace (providence) that they enjoy the abundant blessings of life. These abundant blessings are "extras" that come as a result of being purchased by the blood of Jesus Christ. In accounting language, excess value that arises from a purchase is termed "goodwill." The difference is in who paid the price.

Introduction to Management Accounting

Is work good? Is it good to get up each morning and go to work? Does it benefit us spiritually, mentally, and physically to actively earn a living? The people of Haiti are descendants of Africans forced into slave labor, and they have a saying about work: "If work was good, the white man would have done it." The Bible tells us that work is good because it is a godly activity. *Read Genesis 2:1-3.* Humans were created as creatures of work (Genesis 2:15), as God told man to "work [the Garden of Eden] and take care of it" (NIV). Work gives purpose and meaning to our lives. It is interesting that people of different ages answer the question "Is work good?" differently. Twenty-year-old college students almost always will say "yes," but older students taking evening classes often question the principle as they start looking forward to retirement. What is wrong with playing golf five times a week?

Work With Your Hands

What is the significance of working with your hands? Is working with physical things superior to working mentally in God's eyes? Is physical work of a higher calling or more satisfying? Different cultures will answer these questions differently. In some of the former Soviet nations, only physical work was considered to provide an honest living. Buying low and selling high (merchandising) was not an honorable way to make a living. Even in the United States, trading shares of stock was considered a dishonorable profession until after the Great Depression and the creation of the SEC.[7] *Read 1 Thessalonians 4:11-12.* We are commanded to "work with your hands." Does it make a difference to God if we work with our hands or with our minds?

Transformed Lives, Our Spiritual Product

Consider for a moment the spiritual product we produce—transformed lives. In accounting, material, labor, and overhead go into each product. Spiritually, we can think of the Word of God that became flesh as the material and the work of the Holy Spirit as the labor. *Read John 6:35-45.* As God teaches, He draws us to him in the conversion process. What is our role in the conversion process? Are we also direct labor, or are we indirect labor and part of overhead? Are Christian colleges and church buildings overhead? I would suggest that Christians be considered indirect labor. We are overhead in the process of transforming lives. Evangelism is not salesmanship. Conversion is not our closing the sale. We carry and deliver the message, but God works within each heart to bring about change.

The Goal of Management Accounting: Wealth Creation Through Production

The problem with successful operations is that they can separate us from God; the temptation is to believe that our success is a result of our own power and intellect. *Read Deuteronomy 8:17-20:* "For it is he who gives you the ability to produce wealth" (NIV). Do we live by our own strength and trust in our bank accountants, or do we trust in God? Second Samuel 24 recounts how King David counted the fighting men. God considered this a great trespass because it did not reflect complete trust and dependence upon Him. In this context, accounting once was considered an evil activity.

Is Manufacturing a Godly Activity?

Are we created by a builder to be builders? *Read Genesis 1:31:* "God saw all that he had made, and it was very good" (NIV). God is the ultimate builder. We were created in His image, so we also are created to be builders. From children to adults, people love to construct, weave, and assemble. For some, this is reflected in activities such as gardening or preparing food. For others, this is reflected in physical construction or in the entrepreneurial activity of building a business. Whatever the medium, we love to build.

The Use of Standards

Managerial accounting uses non-financial standards to measure performance. Management and employees (or their unions) often debate these standards. So it is in the spiritual realm. Standards are hotly debated. The timing and meaning of baptism, for example, is one of the most debated standards. Many people say baptism in water is required for salvation (Acts 2:38-41), while others say only grace saves us (Galatians 3:1-9). By what standards does God judge us? *Read Matthew 5:21-22.* Jesus outlines perfection in the so-called "Sermon on the Mount," recorded in Matthew 5–7. What source do you use to determine godly standards?

Activity-Based Costing

The accounting method that assigns cost to a specific activity is called activity-based costing, or ABC. The activities are grouped into cost pools, and each cost pool has a cost driver. Total overhead for the product is determined by the use of each cost pool. The goal of ABC is to eliminate non-value-added activities. The spiritual life includes many activities that contribute to spiritual growth and many that are not value-added, which reduce our spirituality. Like the accounting technique of ABC, we must continually evaluate our activities and determine their costs. *Read Matthew 16:24-28:* "What good will it be for a man if he gains the whole world, yet forfeits his soul?" (NIV). We can be consumed with activities—even good activities that help others—that sacrifice our own time with God. The wise person will discern the difference between life's value-added activities and non-value-added activities.

Questionable Products
Can a faithful Christian produce wine? The answer is "yes" because the Lord Jesus Christ Himself created wine. *Read John 2:1-11.* The Gospel is compared to new wine, and Paul encouraged Timothy to use a little wine for his stomach's sake. But drunkenness is a sin, and the number of lives that have been ruined by excessive consumption is horrific. With alcoholic beverages, people either like the feeling (the "buzz") or they don't. If you like the feeling of losing control, drinking is a problem for you. The production of questionable products falls under the admonition of the Apostle Paul in 1 Corinthians 10:23: " 'Everything is permissible'—but not everything is beneficial" (NIV).

Process Costing or Job-Order Costing or Both?
Does God use a job-order costing system or a process costing system? If sin has a spiritual cost per person, God uses a job-order system. *Read Mark 2:8-12.* We each are accountable for our own sins. What about the sins of a nation? Does God accumulate the sins of a nation and then hold all of the citizens accountable, as in process costing? Do you worry about and pray for forgiveness for the sins of your nation?

[1] ACCOUNTING'S SAINTLY ANCESTRY: The possible Influence of Saint Thomas Aquinas on the Development of Double Entry Accounting, Accounting Through the Eyes of Faith, 2nd edition, compiled by Jack E. Bower, 2002.

[2] HEAVENLY ACCOUNTING: God's Accounting System Revealed Through the Scriptures, Accounting Through the Eyes of Faith, compiled by Jack E. Bower, Eastern College, 2000.

[3] SCRIPTURAL ADMONITION TO STUDY ACCOUNTING, Accounting Through the Eyes of Faith, compiled by Jack E. Bower, Eastern College, 2000.

[4] "Mansion Over the Hilltop" by Ira Stanphill, #881, Songs of Faith & Praise, Alton H. Howard, 1997.

[5] Trueblood, Eton, A Place to Stand, Harper & Row Publishers, N.Y., 1969.

[6] Forbes, July 28, 1997, "The 100 Largest U.S. Multinationals."

[7] "Easy but Sleazy," Bridget O'Brian, Wall Street Journal, Tuesday, May 28, 1996.

Discussion Questions for

Accounting

Through the Eyes of Faith

#1   A bachelors or masters degree in business at many academic institutions would not contain a strong liberal arts component. Why do many of the Christian Colleges such as Eastern University design the business curriculum to include courses on justice and cross-cultural issues? Would this time be better utilized in "pure" business topics like accounting or finance?

#2   Explain the spiritual linkage between Leviticus 25 and Luke 4:21. How is Jesus the personification of the year of Jubilee? Using your knowledge of accounting and finance, why is sin described as a liability account and salvation as the cancellation of debt?

#3   What is the linkage between accounting and justice? Why was the church so concerned about the development of a comprehensive accounting system when economic commerce began to flourish internationally?

#4   International trade can often improve the economic condition of a country and its people. The raising of debt and equity for business ventures in less developed nations is difficult to impossible without an extensive knowledge of financial markets and international accounting standards. Technology is making the task easier, but international accounting standards struggle to find acceptance. How would one universally accepted accounting standard improve the raising of debt and equity for small business ventures around the world?

#5   You are a U.S. citizen and you work for World Vision International in Monrovia CA. You have been out of the U.S. for 350 days during the last tax year. A friend has mentioned that you might not be subject to U.S. income tax because of the length of time you have been away from the U.S. You want to resolve this important tax issue. How would you **begin your research** assuming you do not have access to a U.S. Internal Revenue Office (IRS) or other professional tax preparer? (You are not required to find the correct number of days.)

#6   You are considering doing relief work in a country not currently served by any major relief organizations. You want to create a feeder organization in the United States for the purpose of raising funds for this new relief effort. What are the major financial criteria for public charity status in the United States?

#7   What is the role of the Certified Public Accountant as auditor and/or consultant in the environmental debate? What are the critical environmental issues for auditors? What is the first step in the audit planning process from an environmental perspective?

#8   A Christian friend has just learned that you are enrolled in a business program. They come to you and express their concern that you will be seduced by worldly pleasures and concerns. They wonder how a true Christian can be a good business student or businessperson. How would you explain to your friend your academic interest in pursuing a business degree?

#9   Why do you think there has been so little research conducted that integrates Christianity and accounting? How do you think this absence has affected the development of accounting information?

#10   Why is it important to see the entire world through from spiritual perspective? Why is it critical to think inductively by contrasting and comparing problem situations from a spiritual perspective?